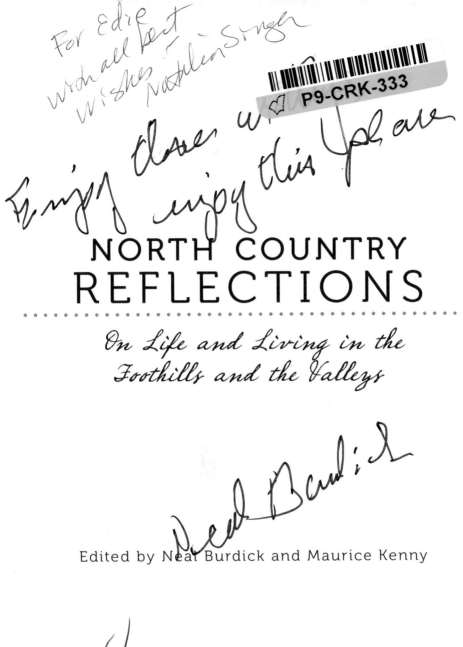

NORTH COUNTRY
REFLECTIONS

On Life and Living in the
Foothills and the Valleys

Edited by Neal Burdick and Maurice Kenny

Charleston · London

THE
History
PRESS

P9-CRK-333

Published by The History Press
Charleston, SC 29403
www.historypress.net

Copyright © 2013 by Neal Burdick and Maurice Kenny
All rights reserved

*Front cover: top, Whit Haynes; middle, Deb MacKenzie; bottom, Barry Lobdell.
Back cover: inset, Tara Freeman; top, Phil Gallos; bottom, Debbie Kanze.*

First published 2013

Manufactured in the United States

ISBN 978.1.62619.115.0

Library of Congress CIP data applied for.

Notice: The information in this book is true and complete to the best of our knowledge. It is offered without guarantee on the part of the author or The History Press. The author and The History Press disclaim all liability in connection with the use of this book.

All rights reserved. No part of this book may be reproduced or transmitted in any form whatsoever without prior written permission from the publisher except in the case of brief quotations embodied in critical articles and reviews.

CONTENTS

CONTENTS

FOREWORD

Here's what I like about this book: it is unabashedly about this place, *this* North Country. No excuses, like "the stories could happen anywhere," or "this is not a work by simply regional writers"—you get the idea. The editors, to their credit, are not ashamed that this volume is about a very specific place and very specific people. It may be true that you could read—and like—this collection on a ranch in Wyoming or in a Manhattan condo, but the book is about *our* place, right here in the Adirondacks and the North Country.

If you've lived here—or visited the region with any regularity—each of these essays will get the bells ringing for you, about wood-splitting or hiking, hobby farms and rural poverty. Some will take you a bit beyond the familiar bells, as Chris Angus does with his very personal look way, way, *way* back into the history of our piece of geography.

I want to upgrade my language: I love this book. It brings together essays by some of our best writers—many of whom I've followed for years, a few I've just met with real delight—all focusing on us, on our place, on this scrabbly rocky bit of ground we drilled our roots into.

Put this book on your nightstand, first. Then move it to the coffee table. Next to the counter in your kitchen, where you perch on a stool while the teakettle water comes to a boil. Keep it moving around the house. Everyone will pick it up and dip in where the bell rings for them.

ELLEN ROCCO
North Country Public Radio
Winter 2013

INTRODUCTION

There was a time when this volume and its twin, *Adirondack Reflections*, were to be one book, with the title *Being: North*. We both felt those two words captured the fact that people live and work, dream and play, suffer and endure—in other words, *exist*—"up here" and captured the essence of where "here" is. But projects grow and evolve when they acquire momentum, and this one expanded in both scope and name.

For a great many years, those who wrote about the region that is the focus of these books were few in number, and they mostly lived elsewhere, only visiting or passing through before retreating to the relative comforts of more urban (and urbane) environments when the weather turned cold and the income grew slim. But beginning with the last quarter of the twentieth century, the region has seen an outpouring of place-based writing by both old hands and newcomers, most of whom have chosen to take up residence, preferring the subtle and often hidden advantages of living in the mountains and rural expanses to the heavily trumpeted disadvantages. It is those writers, some of whom have never been published before, to whom we wished to offer a platform with these books. Aside from the fact that we want you to discover them, we also want them to discover each other.

Many people helped bring these books into being. Foremost among them, of course, are the more than three dozen contributors of written and artistic works. We thank them for sharing their creative talents, for giving of their energy and, above all, for their patience. Special accolades go to Tara Freeman, staff photographer at St. Lawrence University, for her priceless technical assistance with the images.

INTRODUCTION

Whether you label it the North Country or the Adirondacks or some combination of the two, the misshapen chunk of New York State that protrudes northward from Interstate 90, beyond the northernmost mainline of American east–west commerce, is a special place in its own special ways. We hope these two books help you come to understand, appreciate and wonder about it a little more.

NEAL BURDICK
MAURICE KENNY
Mud Season, 2013

Part I
The Land

ECHOES BENEATH THE LAND

By Chris Angus

I once held in my hand a primitive stone point from the Archaic Period, at least two thousand to five thousand years old. It had been unearthed in a garden in the village of Canton overlooking the falls of the Grass River. In that long-ago time, Native Americans had likely had a temporary fishing encampment near the once teeming waters.

The point was six or seven inches long, three inches wide and nearly half an inch thick at its center, with sides carefully chiseled to make an object of great beauty. It was probably intended for use as a spear point or cutting tool, though the anthropologist who allowed me to examine it said he thought it had never been used and might have been intended for ceremonial purposes.

I can no longer drive past that busy village intersection without pondering what it must have been like so long ago when someone left that exquisite point behind. There was likely nothing there at all, except perhaps a primitive fire hearth or racks for drying fish. And the land. The people were indelibly connected to the land back then; they lived off the land. Today we might say they lived off the grid.

Thousands of years ago, everyone lived off the grid, of course. And the spirit and freedom of that way of life still resonates with some in the North Country today. They live in reclaimed farmhouses, self-built log homes or run-down trailers, doing hardscrabble farming, raising a few animals, just getting by. They refuse to shop at Wal-Mart or make monthly payments to the power or cable companies. Windmills, methane, firewood and homemade dams produce power and heat. Some won't own a TV or telephone, listen to National Public Radio or even read a newspaper. I suspect more than a few would make their own spear points, if someone would only show them how.

These people have been born into the wrong time. They remind me of old family friends who packed up everything they owned and moved to Alaska in the 1950s when I was growing up. Irresistibly drawn to wild open spaces, they sought an end to offices, schools, traffic, taxes, bills, even neighbors. I can still see their overloaded Oldsmobile chugging down the highway, rooftop disappearing beneath reams of army surplus tents and sleeping bags. In search of another North Country. In search of what those archaic forebears had.

Could the original Native Americans have thought of this part of the world as the "North" Country? It's hard to imagine, really. They were so tied to the land that such a term may not have occurred to them. They moved with the seasons, with the game, berries and fish runs. Perhaps they saw "the Northern Lands" as regions where the air turned colder and winter lingered longer. North, south, east, west—one suspects it was all just "the land" to them: one great, all-encompassing natural wonder.

The Paleo-Indian hunters who preceded their archaic descendants left their own projectiles along the shores of the inland sea, now Lake Champlain, eleven thousand years ago. Their spear points were larger than their followers', a decrease in weapon size that corresponds with the extinction, around 8000 BC, of the caribou, bison and mammoth. The Woodland cultures that followed these first primitive inhabitants left behind smaller points still, along with a handful of dugout canoes, stone gouges, axe heads, pipes and pestles.

That ancient spear point found in the village of Canton is just one remnant of past worlds that still echo in North Country culture. The rolling farmland and Adirondack foothills are dotted with other reminders: mills, iron forges, defunct canals, quarries, lead mines, corduroy roads, enormous barns and the elaborate Victorian homes of successful lumbermen or railroad men.

The barns are disappearing quickly, sinking into the landscape or being taken apart for their lumber. I watched one well-known round barn outside of Potsdam, a spectacular bit of craftsmanship, deteriorate over a decade, as it languished, enveloped in a property dispute. Today, it is gone, preserved only in a few photographs. But many of those elegant Victorian homes remain. A few of the mills have been turned into restaurants or preservation societies. A handful of iron manufactories like the one at Rossie still have standing stone walls and chimneys to remind us of once-vibrant communities that are now silent. The corduroy roads have disappeared beneath the soil, along with many of the thick stone walls of long-forgotten canal locks.

The arrival of the Amish brought renewal to many old homesteads, farms and sawmills, along with the revival of a disappearing way of life. Similarly, the rise of a conservationist ethic led to the protection of remnants of the wilderness, of our rivers in their natural state and of wildlife. Craftspeople, too, preserve many of the old ways, building guide boats, carving animal and bird figures, weaving rugs and baskets, growing organic produce and making cheese, bacon, honey and many other products in time-honored fashion.

Someone I once knew described people in search of this sort of renewal, of a more primitive way of life, as dead-enders, a term most recently associated with the hardcore supporters of Saddam Hussein, who kept the Iraq war going on principle even when all seemed lost. But I think what my friend was getting at was that many present-day off-the-gridders simply enjoy being contrary and living beyond the beaten path. Their ambitions and goals have little to do with modern society. They seek to hang on to values and skills that they respect and to something that often goes along with that—solitude. Where better to find it than on a dead-end road? Hardly anyone drives down a dead-end road, except by accident.

I've been exploring out-of-the-way places in the North Country for many years. A dead-end sign is nothing so much as an invitation, a magnet pulling me forward to an unknown destination. There's no telling what one will find once these mostly dirt roads peter out. Perhaps a ramshackle homestead, barns of all sizes collapsing in on themselves, a ferocious dog careening toward the car, ancient and inscrutable farm machinery littering rock-filled cow pastures, along with battered cars, school buses, old appliances and piles of tires.

But equally often, a modern home will have supplanted that old farmhouse, a huge McMansion sprouting satellite dishes, fenced-in swimming pools, elaborate jungle gyms and expensive plantings. My brother-in-law finds such places distasteful. He prefers the old ways, keeping venerable collections of "possibles" about his home, piles of lumber and metal that may one day prove useful. He once came up with an idea for a new lawn ornament for the modern, suburban homes that have been taking over America's backcountry. Instead of those silhouetted forms of moose or laid-back plywood farmers that sometimes sprout from front yards, his plan was to create cutouts of old, wrecked cars and refrigerators that one could stick in the ground. Voila! Instant North Country. A reality check that would remind passers-by of the "good old days."

Veterans are sometime residents of the back of beyond, happily gridless and eager to stay away from people who have never experienced PTSD.

Who can question their desire to escape from what they experienced at war and from its aftermath, the injuries and neglect and memories? Good for them. Getting, and staying, away from it all is an essential part of the American spirit. If we all followed that spirit, leaving people alone, avoiding preemptive wars of choice, perhaps we might have need for fewer veterans.

Which is not to say that the North Country is a dead end. To the contrary. It can still offer an example of life as it once was, slower paced, less hassled, neighbors helping each other out, open land. The North Country still offers the lure of a new beginning. That is what brought the Amish, though they sometimes clash with their more modern neighbors over the use of buggies on dark country roads, over laws that make them pay taxes and follow building codes, over their view of what proper medical procedures should be. But their independent way of life touches something in all of us and enriches by its example. Their plain, well-kept homes sometimes jar with a neighbor's rundown or ill-kempt one. There seems almost a cleanness of spirit that emanates from the Amish.

That spirit reflects our long-ago archaic spear-maker, who was also connected to the land, though in a more fluid manner. He did not live in a house, which, as the late comedian George Carlin said, "is just a place to keep your stuff." If those ancient hunters had stayed in one spot, it's hard to imagine their front yards filling with the daily detritus of their lives. Because for those early Americans, each belonging had a purpose, maybe even a spirit, and they would no more throw away a broken arrow or chipped spear point than they would the carcass of a caribou. It is one reason my anthropologist friend believes that buried spear point was disposed of for some ceremonial purpose. It would never have simply been discarded.

The archaic "possibles pile" would have been instantly recycled into something useful. Just as the Amish turn garden and food waste into compost and hundred-year-old farm machinery into parts for plowing, ancient cultures wasted nothing. Of course, the natural materials they drew from didn't wear out like a washing machine or a junked car, becoming piles of useless junk. Rather, at the end of its functional life, virtually any object could become compost or firewood or, at the very least, a buried ceremonial object. Perhaps that is what our landfills today really are, ceremonial repositories of our culture.

It's not hard to imagine our descendants, one thousand years hence, digging up a plastic child's toy, a titanium tennis racket or the remnants of a rusted Oldsmobile and waxing rhapsodic about their finds, as I have about that archaic point. Distance and time can give something absolutely ordinary a new sheen. There is a place where I go canoeing where I can stare down into the water and see cedar posts that are remnants of an old cofferdam from the 1800s. Trace bits of red paint still remain, though it would not have been necessary to preserve the posts. An ordinary bit of nineteenth-century infrastructure every bit as common as that long ago ceremonial point. But the effect on today's observer, a combination of respect for craft and awe at its endurance, would likely not have been felt by its creators any more than today's laborers who lay down a fresh topping of asphalt are likely to ponder the significance of their work in the great arc of human advancement.

Near that cofferdam, there is a channel I paddle down that was constructed more than one hundred years ago by horses scraping out the earth with great buckets. This waterway, cut as a passage for floating logs to market, is clearly not natural as it cuts straight as an arrow for over a quarter of a mile, in stark contrast to the winding river. It is yet another remnant of lost infrastructure. Today's loggers prefer machines that cut, strip and stack the logs and even helicopters to transport them out of the backcountry.

All human endeavor builds upon what came before, whether buildings, political systems, philosophies, legal structures, scientific theories or technologies. As our own North Country moves deeper into the twenty-first century, we do so on the legacies of our forebears. And strangely enough, one of those legacies today seems to be a growing awareness that the old ways are not necessarily something to be discarded or cast aside. That they can be built upon and added to is a given, as we have built upon and added to those things the ancient Greek philosophers gave us, a legal system and a method of thought. But there can also be intrinsic value in objects like that ancient spear point and in time-honored ways of doing things.

We learn more every year about the ways that our ever-expanding populations and industries have damaged the world. More and more of us are beginning to realize that the Amish, our pioneer settlers and even those archaic forebears have much to teach us about not just preserving the old ways but using them to diminish our collective impact on the landscape. Small-scale and organic farming are celebrating a rebirth, as are new technologies to create and better use energy. The North Country is home to many such efforts.

On a crisp autumn afternoon, I walk down yet another dead-end road, past laboriously crafted stone fences outlining lonely pastures slowly returning to woodland. Amid a stand of ancient, gnarled oak trees, I pause and stare into a crumbling foundation. It is constructed of sandstone carved from one of many defunct quarries that dot the North Country. Weeds tug at stones that seem lost somehow, their function no longer urgent. But in one corner, someone has begun to remove the thick, rectangular slabs and pile them for later retrieval. These stones, it seems, will soon be reborn as someone's fireplace, walkway or even home.

The remnants of our past, like those crumbling Greek structures, have much to offer, much to teach us still. We would do well to listen to the echoes from beneath the land.

THE LURE OF THE ST. LAWRENCE

By R.L. Cardarelli

When I was a boy, my Uncle Joe took me fishing out of Henderson Harbor, a small community on the banks of Eastern Lake Ontario. We fished near the Galloo Islands. Smallmouth black bass fishing was exceptional, and it drew people from all over the country. I never forgot that first experience: the beauty of the lake and islands and the thrill of catching (on a fly rod) bass that danced on sparkling and shimmering water.

Later, when I had my own family, my wife and I decided to purchase a grand boat—a thirty-two-foot Chris-Craft twin screw, inboard weekender—instead of a new home with a formal dining room. We introduced our two boys to fishing on the St. Lawrence River and Lake Ontario. They were about the same age as I was when I first fished the North Country: eleven and twelve years old.

Our boat was docked at Anchor Marina in Cape Vincent. Carved out of limestone bedrock, it's a safe haven for pleasure craft. A large break wall also protects this stretch of shoreline. It is sometimes used to tie up the tugboats and barges that frequently ply the St. Lawrence River.

At that time, our home and business were in Rochester, New York. On weekends we were drawn to our boat in the Cape. The serenity and natural beauty of the area, along with the great fishing, was a shared family experience that we all benefited from and cherished.

When our sons were no longer anxious to spend weekends with us, we decided to sell the cruiser and buy a smaller boat and later some land for a new home in the North Country. The land, on which we built a home on the banks of the St. Lawrence, gives us nearly the same view as we had from our docked cruiser. To the north is Wolfe Island; to the northeast, Carleton Island. In summer, they are lush with vegetation and frame this fractional expanse of water where the St. Lawrence meets Lake Ontario.

In the North Country, the St. Lawrence River stands out more than any other aspect of the natural environment. It is always beautiful, open and fascinating. Each season has its special natural phenomena. In spring, Canada geese return, and the fly-over is awesome and inspiring to hear and see. Summer is, for many, the premier season. The vegetation is lush and green. The temperature is comfortable, and for the most part, breezes are plentiful. Come fall, the weather cools and is more unpredictable. The full green of summer gives way to reds, yellows and browns as the leaves fall and cover the landscape. Nature slows; so does the rhythm of human activity. Deer hunting and muskie fishing quicken the pace a bit, but these activities are short-lived. Once the trees have lost their leaves, more of the vast open areas can be viewed. It is this openness, this lack of population density, that allows North Country people to enjoy their natural surroundings and sense of freedom. Nature is always nearby. When winter takes over, the river becomes a playground for ice fishing, snowmobiling, cross-country skiing and trekking. The open white expanse is beautiful to behold.

Probably the most prevalent criticism of North Country living comes in the question-statement: "Isn't it very cold in the winter?" My answer is delivered in the form of a poem I wrote one wintry day:

White Wind

At sixteen degrees below zero
The wind is white.
I am awed by such a wondrous winter sight.
Trees lightly covered
With the finest white mist
Of the season.
Only a quiet
Compelling beauty
Gives this frigid scene
A delight
....Beyond reason.

The agrarian aspect of the North Country adds to this feeling of openness. Dairy farming is prevalent, thanks to the abundance of grassland.

It is also not uncommon to see sheep or horses grazing and romping in large pastures. The proximity of these farms to villages, towns and small cities is characteristic of northern living. You are never far removed from what is generally considered rural when you live in this part of New York State. Consequently, those of us who live here are often thought of as "country folk." I guess that's agreeable to us.

Generally, North Country folk, full-time or part-time, recognize the unique rugged natural beauty that surrounds them. It continues to exist largely because civilization hasn't completely caught up with this region. For some that is a blessing, for others it is a handicap. The retired folk don't need employment, but others do and job opportunities are scarce. Like many endeavors, living in the North Country involves taking the bitter with the sweet. At my three-quarter-century milestone in 2009, I am fortunate to feel that life in this part of America is indeed mostly sweet.

Vision

I've never seen the grass so green
or
Maple leaves blowing in the breeze
or
Rain drops making circles in puddles
or
Birds gathering at a feeder in huddles
Why not?
Maybe, I was too busy looking for all those other things I got.

I find the natural environment in the North Country inspirational and wonderful to be a part of and to enjoy. For some, living in this area can be a challenge and a chore. Witness the population growth in the South and Southwest. The reasons for this migration are many: lower heating bills, greater employment opportunities, ease of travel, modern conveniences, diverse cultural activities. All these positive aspects of so-called "easy living" can lead to population density. The infestations of over-civilization have not yet reached and obscured the natural wonder of the North Country. Thankfully, the North Country retains its rugged character. Nature is not only recognized and respected but also enjoyed—and not by too many.

NIGHT WALK

By Rick Henry

D arkness brings its own kind of movement. Deer brave the yard. A skunk will pass. The fox that lounges, basking in the sun down on the rocks by the willow by the creek, leaves its footprints in the muddy paddocks. Horses generally move the same—steady grinding until the hay is gone and then a quasi lock-legged doze between shifting weight and swishing tails, swishing mixed with a quick flick and stomp. Entertainment for the deerflies as they settle in, making way for the night bugs. Missing are the squeal and kicks, the heavy flirting over the fence. In the back paddocks, those closest to the woods, the wilds, the horses are likely to start and whirl, prance and blow, given the specter of monsters in the bushes, in the trees.

Roxanne called after dusk. Early August with the ground giving off its heat to the night even as the western sky continued to glow. Tula and Sable weren't in the paddock. The gate was open. They weren't in the yard. The gate was open. She'd said it twice, as if they might have picked a lock. Much as horses are prone to destroying fence, splintering boards, chewing posts, fences are held by their goodwill.

Staring out the window watching winter's movement, dark at five and snow, fat flakes in the light cast by the halogen yard light, staring out the window without a hint of surprise—that twenty-five horses are starving up in Lisbon, living outside in the sub-zero, eating the walls of the barn, eating their own manure and respecting the fence as the temperature drops, as sores develop and fester, as a foal worries a mare for milk—fences are held by goodwill. One could open their gate, let them out, let them into the night for a bit of a night walk.

Fences are honored by goodwill, which is why Tula and Sable began their night walk through an unlatched gate. It was difficult to imagine them walking into the farmyard, up to the house and across the road to a hayfield. Much easier to imagine them turning toward the river, down between the paddocks, where Token, Dutch and Cooper on the left and Velvet and Scala on the right were steadily grinding their teeth against hay. In the back paddock, Jesse must have started at their appearance, or not. Tula and Sable hadn't come from the woods; they were probably grazing their way down the alley. They were an unlikely pair. Tula, a large Belgian mare, blonde mane, and the delight of all the little girls, was generally quiet. She could, on occasion, get quite full of herself, spin and whirl with the best of the quarter horses, perhaps because she grew up with one. She was a rescue. Her leg had had its own open sore, cut to the bone, leaving her unable to stand without the sharp-booted kicks of her owner. Sable was a dark thoroughbred. She was older. Generally quiet, quiet enough for the little girls to ride, but sometimes a bit witchy with the rest of the mares. At the time, she had an eye infection and was wearing an eye mask to keep off the flies.

At night, with an alley full of grass. With the boys on the left and girls on the right, they would have been nose to the ground, eating the fresh green grass that was just collecting early evening dew. Which of them took the next step first? Which turned the corner and kept walking?

At the end of the alley, the trail is five feet wide to the left. Down a ways past the arena, the gelding's pasture is on the left on the other side of a thickish "row" of trees and rubber fence. River on the right, down a steep embankment held by honeysuckles and hawthorns.

It isn't so wide to the right, down to the culvert through which runs Van Rensselaer Creek. Odd for a creek to be named after the Dutch so close to the St. Lawrence. Odd for a creek, barely a creek, to be named at all. The rivers, the Grass(e), the Raquette, bear the burden of the French. Could a creek hold fast a Dutch name from over one hundred years earlier? It cuts through the lower mares' pasture, under a fence and through soft ground before running through the culvert, into the marsh, fanning out and to the Little River. Just over the culvert is a slight rise to a gate—the cabin pasture. It's perhaps two acres, fenced with rubber. Traces of barbed wire where it touches a seep of an acre—cattails and winterberries. It has four gates all told. Turn left along a foot trail, rooted, rising, dipping, through a slight bleed. In August, the entire world is little more than water moving about. In January, it's ice—dangerously so. Then, the cabin. The river is just below. If Tula and Sable had gone that way, they would have turned right at the cabin rather than cross the river. Dana and Roxanne went to the right, down and over the culvert and left along the foot trail next to the cabin pasture. I went to the left and could hear them calling as I walked behind the arena—"Tu-la," "Sable." Beyond the arena and the thickish row of trees and the rubber fence.

We talk as the snow falls. Inside is warm. We know nothing about the fences in Lisbon other than they are board, bits of electric, and strung with baling twine. We know nothing about how big the paddock is. There is a rumor that a blue tarp, behind the barn but visible from down the road a piece, covers a dead horse. We know nothing about what surrounds the paddock. The road on one side, yes. But fields? Pastures? Woods?

Goodwill, of course, is relative. Two horses, sold back in Sable's time, sold and relocated to their new owners' homes, willed themselves back. Freckles, a gray with small spots of brown all over, flea-bitten, was bought by a young girl out toward Pyrites, a girl who owned a paint named Dollar. Dollar could pick a lock and opened the gate-latch at will. One day, Freckles stepped through and came on, seven miles at a trot, followed by a man in an old Cougar or Impala, a man who was kindly keeping an eye on him until help could arrive. We could see Freckles coming down Barnes Road; we could hear metal shoes on macadam, which was for the better. Seven miles at a trot would have wreaked a small havoc on unshod hooves. He stayed on the road rather than cutting across the field, ignored the stop sign and rounded the corner, came past the house-side drive to the second drive and in, looping back and along the arena. He stopped in the middle barnyard. He blew out. The paddocks were all wrong, having been redesigned, one hundred tons of sand, new posts, new boards, new fence. Wilkie and Jack in the back paddock lifted their heads and returned to stray strands of hay. Everest, in the front, pranced a little. Blew out. Turned. Kicked out. Feet nearly taking the top board. Freckles blew out. Across the alley, the mares...Holly flagged her tail. But Holly would flag. Would pee. Bring on the boys, she says. Squeals and stomps. The Cougar, or Impala, gave up the chase, relieved that he didn't have to do anything. How many farms had Freckles passed along the way? The man in the Cougar, or Impala, must have been hoping each one was *the* one.

The e-mail reports are heartbreaking. The worst came with photographs, including a mare with an abscess on her back hip that is open and oozing. It has been that way since October, the e-mail says. The gelding wasn't shown, but described: "Topline sagging like an old barn ready to collapse into itself. The rain rot along top has become one enormous scab-like crust." It's the easiest thing in the world to starve a horse.

Rudy, another thoroughbred, came up Meade Road, running along the side berm looking for the back way in, one that would bring him home across the river. He knew the path was there but couldn't find it. He was finally caught by a friend who offered him a Nutra Bar and held on, waiting for Dana, a lead rope and a can of grain. He didn't make it "home" that time. Instead, he was led back to the fence he'd broken and through it into the barn and a stall. He took a different route on subsequent jail breaks and made it all the way back to his boys before a return-trip by trailer.

Booker, up on Waterman Hill, a thoroughbred off the track, busted fence from fear. The sudden appearance of cows and the jolt of electric, and he was off, through the fence, onto the road, which might as well have been a racetrack. He only made eight-tenths of a mile at a full gallop before pulling up, race over. Cows will do that to a horse, to a thoroughbred. Anything will do that to a thoroughbred. The "pulling up" probably bought him an early retirement. He stood in the middle of the road, one big nerve, laced with veins. Dripping water. The lead rope that found him was a lifeline.

The Lisbon horses are different, however. The two in the worst shape, the mare and the gelding, could have broken a fence, but only if they'd fallen on it. Only if they'd gotten close enough to it. Neither could have gotten close. The mare has a deep puncture wound on her haunch. The gelding's feet haven't been trimmed in so long that it is nearly impossible to walk. He's lucky, all things considered. There was a farm out toward Russell where the animals were neglected. A pig died, feet frozen in the mud so he couldn't move. Over in Potsdam, a man in his twenties was caught throwing kittens at a tree as if they were baseballs. It's the easiest thing in the world to starve a horse.

Roxanne and Dana calling. Their Tu-las and Sa-bles faded as they passed the cabin, as I walked to the left. The air was still. Leaves were still. I could hear a pickup truck from as far as the Kunoco Station. It slowed, stopped at the blinking four-way. The river, on the right, deepened, noise over rocks and shallows left upstream. The trout were no doubt hovering just under the surface waiting for the evening mosquitoes, deerfly, other insects. The pickup passed the gelding pasture and accelerated past the house, up past the Brick Chapel and over the hill. There was the quick sound of tires over the bridge, and it was gone. If I had been at treetop, I probably could have heard the traffic on Route 11, out by the Pizza Hut, Stewarts and the P&C. I might have heard Roxanne and Dana calling as they stepped gingerly through the ooze. I wondered, idly, if they were wearing boots.

I strained, foot quiet, listening for a steady munching, teeth grinding grass. Tula and Sable would have had to have broken through the rubber fence to get into the geldings' pasture. The river veered away on the right. So did the rubber fence on the left. A dip through a more wooded space, a small creek, a kill, maybe, or something smaller, something unnamed, through a small culvert. The water there works itself over rocks, barely loud enough to cover the sound of horses' teeth on grass. Not loud enough to cover a snort, the quiet blowing out of dust or pollen.

The fence returned on the left, string now. Electric string. The tiniest of humming coming from the power lines that cut through the property. A sharp turn to the right, and over a larger culvert, another creeklet, rivulet, all marshes bleeding toward the river. A small clearing. A steady hum from above. Around the two-rail jump. Feet quiet. Night quiet. Road oddly quiet. And, finally, into the field alight with the stars and hundreds of fireflies.

Aside from a narrow trail to the right just after the jump, there is no place for a horse, let alone a draft horse, to veer from the path. It's a good half mile to the field.

Sitting on a stump. Listening. The fireflies part, as if mist, as if something large were coming through. As if ghost horses.

There are rumors, confirmed, of people who just can't deal with horses, the expense of hay, the constant watering, of people just opening the gates allowing the horses to escape, to leave, to wander the world. Annie told a story at the feed store about nearly hitting one as she drove home. Thought it was a deer about to cross the road and swerved, nicked the far white line before swinging back into her lane. Only later did she think "horses." The blacksmith knows the rumors and can sort for truth. The horses were all shod, he told us. Less of an angle to the front and a toe clip on the shoe, which suggests someone from the southern Adirondacks, from the area surrounding Old Forge. He's unusually quiet about the name. Annie didn't know about the shoes, but she heard one of the mares was wearing a rain sheet. She said they were just grazing by the side of the road, out 310, not a farm within ten miles knew anything about them. It was as though there was no escape, no broken fences, no unlatched gates. It was as though someone came to a stop with a gooseneck stock horse trailer, opened the doors and gave them a shove before locking up and driving off. Too expensive to keep. Hay prices rising. One imagines that they first opened the gates. Took down the fences. And still the horses stayed. Waiting for the next bale they knew would come. Some stories come third-hand. Friend of a friend trailers her horse to Otter Creek. She parks. She heads out on the trails, on the buckle, her horse has been there before. When she returns, horses are tied to her trailer. No trucks, no trailers in sight.

There's the horses starving in Lisbon, a nice-looking wagon-load of hay twenty-five feet on the other side of a paddock fence. There's Tula and Sable caught, on the wrong side, sweet-talking through flouted noses as Roxanne and Dana come along, through a bramble of raspberries, through a slight gap in the fence, open the last of the four fences to the cabin pasture. It must have been Tula in the lead, Tula taking them through the woods. Sable's eye infection and fly mask too much for her to take the front, unless their path was from memory. Roxanne and Dana opening the last gate. The horses know their way and walk ahead, through the cabin pasture, then over the culvert and back to the barn, easy as can be.

Sable is with the Kays, now. Retired and on pasture. Tula is twenty-three. She occasionally takes day walks—through an open gate, down through the barn, out, down the alley for a few bites of grass and maybe back through.

Darkness brings its own kind of movement. Winter. Woodstove ablaze. It is, in this drafty old farmhouse, still warmer inside than it is out. The movement is mostly in the pacing. The sitting. The standing up again. In the waiting. We're expecting the call that will alert us to the delivery of two of the Lisbon horses. The two in the worst shape. The one with a deep wound that has sent shivers of sympathy across the 'net as a photograph accompanies each forwarded e-mail. The other simply starved into stillness. Topline caving. Rain rot like a shell. So say the SPCA and the vet. We're waiting for the call that lets us know that two of the starving horses will find their way to our barn. Dark, and now, waiting for darkness's own kind of movement. Should they come, there will be the starts and whirls, prances and blows, given the specter of ghost horses in the yard. Should they come, we will walk them down to the barn through the dark and the snow.

APPLES, SARDINES AND BULLHEAD

By Betsy Kepes

I'm walking fast, tearing through a dark hemlock woods on my way to the river. If I don't keep moving, I'm afraid I'll explode. It's my first day of a two-week stint as caretaker for my father, and I'm angry at myself for resenting the responsibility. Am I some kind of monster child?

By the time I'm pushing through the brush to the river's edge I'm calmer. It won't be that bad. He's a lovable old man, even if he can't remember to take his medications and he's not sure if he ate lunch and his body now hunches forward as he shuffles along on legs that have lost their feeling below the knees.

The Grass River here is wide and majestic, a dark flow of water on its way to the rapids in the village of Canton. I stand on the rocky shore for a long time, watching the brown water push against a fallen tree and listening to leaves rustle with an end-of-summer dryness. It won't be so bad.

The farm had been on the market for over a year when my parents bought it in 1978. The spectacular property, only a mile south of the village of Canton, included a farmhouse, a big red barn, fifty acres of loamy fields, one hundred acres of mature woods and thirty acres of swamp, plus a long stretch of river frontage. The price tag was steep though, high enough that the locals laughed. What did they think, those folks from New Jersey? People around here don't pay that kind of money for land.

My mother kept her eye on the place. She'd been cross-country skiing in the woods at the farm and remembered the beauty of the widely spaced sugar maples and black cherry. She'd always been happy living in the village, but this place called out to her. It didn't take much to convince my dad.

He wanted to plant a bigger garden, and he'd never owned much land. After a year they made an offer, half of the asking price. At first there was silence, but within months the property traded hands. My family of six, plus a dog, moved out of a skinny Victorian on a narrow lot in town to a white farmhouse in the country.

It's almost warm enough to swim on this mild September day. A dip in the cool river would certainly clear my head. I wonder how many years it's been since my father waded into the brown water here. He used to roam these woods with a bow saw, clearing trails and making elegant little stacks of firewood out of smooth beech saplings. He wasn't interested in practical wood-getting and never used a chainsaw. Much like Thoreau, he made a living with words, in his case as a professor of English. He bought firewood from others and saved the big trees here from the sawmill. For him, these woods are a treasured resource, not to be disturbed.

I've inherited that reverence for wild places and the composure they can bring to a mind that is fretting. After an hour of walking I'm calmer, and I even have a wildlife sighting to share with my father. I'd taken a trail upriver and then circled back through a young woods and a stunted Scotch pine plantation. Breaking back out into the open, at the end of a long narrow field that always makes me think of a barnstormer's runway, I'd seen a flash of movement. A deer, I assumed. But something about the gait wasn't right. When it arced toward the woods I saw its tail—long and bushy—and the unmistakable outline of a coyote. I watched it lope along the open ground with an easy stride. It ran away from me, but not in a panic like a deer. This animal was comfortable here, and I was a temporary hindrance. After I passed through, it would be back, nosing around in the recently cut grass, looking for rodents displaced, or killed, by the brush hog.

My dad is sitting on the back deck when I walk past the barn and the vegetable garden, a weedy ruin that would have embarrassed him ten years ago. His garden never had the least green of a weed; the raised beds he filled with vegetables of prizewinning stature. He did all the spading by hand, spending hours turning over the heavy loam and pulling weeds. He'd pocket bits of glass and crockery he found in the dirt, and once he found a stone axe head, a dark polished rock with a sharp wedge on one end. He liked to show it to visitors, an ancient tool from the first farmers on the land.

"Hey, Dad!"

He looks up, locates my voice and smiles.

"Let's pick some apples."

I go inside to find some bags while he's attempting to stand up. It's tough getting out of a chair when your legs are unreliable, and he's too proud to ask for help. He's eighty-two and stooped, but he's still a tall man, well over six feet. If he falls, my mother doesn't have the strength to help him up. I'm hoping I do.

We walk slowly across the yard to the apple trees. I've already scouted it out, and it is wonderful to see my father's face light up when he sees the huge red apples on one tree and gigantic yellow ones on another. Maybe he's walked here already this fall, but to him the big apples are new again, a splendid surprise.

"We have a good crop this year," Dad says, and stops to admire the trees. I know enough not to ask him what the varieties are. He wouldn't have known even before his memory became weak. My mother ordered young trees from a catalog, and my father dug deep holes, added compost and put the new trees into the ground. The tags announcing their variety faded in the sun, and no one thought to care. Some of the trees succumbed to rodents and disease, a few were replaced and others grew into these gnarly trees loaded with fruit.

I suggest he pick the high red apples while I get the ones on the lower branches. He hangs on to the tree for balance and drops the big apples into a plastic grocery bag I hold out. A couple times, he tips and I hold my breath, but he grabs a branch and pretends nothing has happened.

The yellow tree is more difficult for him. It's bigger, with a thick trunk and a wide umbrella of branches, nipped off clean at the height of a deer's mouth. There's not as much to hang on to and he sways, uncertain.

"Let's leave some for the deer," he says.

I'm not feeling that generous, but I can see he's had enough. We've filled five grocery bags. This weekend I'll get his grandkids to climb into the trees and shake the branches, a chore they will love.

We sit together on the deck, each of us with a cutting board and a paring knife. It's still warm; a flannel shirt is enough on this sunny fall day. I tell my father to cut the apples in quarters, then those pieces in half. We'll make applesauce and put most of it in the freezer. It will please my mother to know we didn't let the apples rot or, more likely, be eaten by the deer.

Preparing the apples is good work for us to do together. I worry at first that my dad will cut himself, but his hands are steady. When we switch to peeled apples, cut in thin slices for apple crisp, he doesn't do as well. His peelings are thick and awkward and his slices uneven. I watch him try to peel an apple in one long swirling curlicue of yellow skin. He was a master at this and delighted us by putting the skin back together to present us with a hollow apple. Today he gives up after the first half circle and returns to his awkward chipping away of the skin. Neither of us says anything about the failure.

He's failing at so much now. The diabetes he's had for fifteen years is affecting his brain—memory loss—and his legs—no feeling in his feet.

"I do believe I have the most beautiful backyard in the world," Dad says, gesturing out to the first field, planted in neat rows of soybeans. Beyond that is the pond and the slope that rises above it where the forest begins. The bright September light makes everything look clean and shiny.

I nod. Once a friend told me my father had a wonderful joie de vivre. It was true, and it still is. I'm grateful that the dementia has, for now at least, created a kind of amnesia. He doesn't fret that he can't walk or garden or read a serious book or even turn on the TV. Those skills are gone, but he finds joy in other things. Every morning he shuffles over to the front window in the kitchen to peer out and admire the giant maple tree in the front yard. And every afternoon he smiles at the wide view of the sunset he can see from the back of the house.

He can still feel anger though. He doesn't like it that my mother has arranged "babysitters" for him while she is away in Alaska visiting my sister and her family. She left behind a schedule on the kitchen counter, and it bothers my father.

"I'm embarrassed," he tells me, putting down his knife. "Joan's not even here, and she's still trying to control me."

I attempt to change the subject, but it's true that he's been given a tight schedule. Each night someone is supposed to arrive to take him out to dinner. They have been instructed to let my father pay with his credit card. Tonight Ward Geddes, a retired Japanese language professor, is on the guest list.

"I don't want to go out for dinner tonight." He sounds stubborn, like a child.

I keep peeling apples, searching for something to say to change the subject.

"I'm going to make dinner for Ward. I'm going to make leek and potato soup." His voice sounds confident now.

This used to be one of his "signature" recipes. My mother insisted he take over some of the dinner-making responsibilities when he retired, and this was one of the meals he could do well. In the garden he carefully tended leeks, starting them inside and transplanting them, like fragile green hairs, into the garden. Scrupulously weeded, watered and manured, the leeks grew huge, their thick bulbs under the mounded soil a creamy white.

But now he can't garden or cook a meal, except to open a can.

He falters. "I'm not sure I have any leeks."

I hate seeing him confused like this.

"Dad, why don't I get Chinese takeout? Then no one has to cook."

This seems an acceptable compromise, and we keep cutting up apples until I glance at my watch and realize I'll be late for my afternoon of teaching piano lessons unless I leave immediately. I rush off, telling him I'll be back about five and we'll finish the apple crisp. We'll serve it for dessert, with ice cream, an American finish to an Oriental meal.

As I drive into town, I hope he'll be okay. Last year he wanted to make coffee but put the entire plastic coffee maker on a burner instead of the Pyrex coffee pot. Fortunately my mother was home and rushed to the kitchen when she smelled burning plastic. Another time, when he had a slight fever and hadn't eaten lunch, he collapsed on the kitchen floor. When my mother arrived home an hour later, his whole body was shaking and he couldn't speak.

I'd be very anxious about leaving except that I know Don Dean will stop by to check his "trap line." My parents hire Don to help with chores that they can no longer do. His work lets them remain proudly independent. Don's been trying to get rid of the rats and chipmunks that have invaded the house. When he checks his traps, he'll also, discreetly, check on my dad.

I hurry to pack up after my last lesson, and when I turn into my parents' driveway a few minutes after five o'clock, Ward's car is already there. I hope Dad has remembered to offer him a beer, maybe even open up a bag of chips. I realize I never called Ward to tell him of our change of plans.

The back door, the only one that anyone uses, pushes open with a squeak. The two old men sit together at a corner of the dining room table. I see plates and glasses.

"Hi, Ward!" I sound very cheerful, I hope.

My father has his back to the door. He's sitting up unusually straight, a sitting-in-church stiffness. "We're having dinner here," he says. "I didn't feel like going out." His voice is clipped.

"I see."

And I do. On the plates the men each have a soupy portion of canned baked beans. Next to the beans glint the bodies of little silver fish—sardines. On the table is half a loaf of bread, the sourdough my husband made and left as a gift, almost a week ago. It must be tough as shoe leather by now.

Ward is being polite, though he laughs nervously when my father asks if he wants seconds. "I was looking forward to going out for a good dinner. This is…"

My father interrupts him, looking fierce. "I didn't say this was a good dinner. But I didn't want to go out."

"Good thing we peeled all those apples." It seems wise to change the subject. I rush around the kitchen looking for ingredients to make a topping for the apple crisp. Flour, oats, sugar. Where does Mom keep her cinnamon? The whole time I'm cooking I'm chatting with Ward, trying to make this seem like a relaxed dinner party.

After I slide the apple crisp into the oven I suggest we take a break before dessert and walk down to the pond. All of us are relieved to have something to do.

We walk slowly past the garden and a weedy, fenced-in corner by the barn that used to be the chicken run. The hens would cluster by the fence when anyone walked by, hoping for carrot tops or table scraps. We joked that my father spoiled his chickens so much that he'd tuck them into bed. This was almost true. He'd often go into the coop at night to make sure all the fat, glossy birds were on their roosts, gathering up any that needed an assist.

The field behind the house stretches to the west and even in the late afternoon it is still bright. For years my parents let a neighboring farmer hay the fields. When that farm went under, they paid another farmer to come in every couple of years to brush hog the land to keep it open. The brush hogging wasn't cheap, so when an ambitious young farmer asked if he could plant crops in the fields, they considered the idea. Would he use chemical fertilizer and pesticides? Yes, but as little as possible. And he'd rotate crops—corn, oats, soybeans.

I think of that conversation now. The fields are in soybeans this year, and the long curved rows are elegant—rounded green plants separated by strips of bare soil. Their beauty dims when I realize these are genetically modified soybeans, a Monsanto invention with leaves that survive when sprayed with RoundUp, an herbicide that kills every other green plant it comes in contact with. Now the scene seems slightly alien, the green too bright, the blank soil too empty. In places where the deer have nipped off leaves, I imagine them chewing up the herbicide residue, a bitter coating on the leaves.

The pond is only a quarter mile from the house, accessible by a rough, grassy road left open between the soybeans. It's tricky ground for my father to walk on. I'm glad he's brought his walking stick; most of the time he says he doesn't need one. When he does use it, we make sure not to call it a cane.

The pond wasn't here when my parents bought the land. It was a low spot at the base of the hill, an intermittent stream flowing through it. When my grandfather died, my father used inheritance money to hire pond builders. The finished product is a work of art—a deep clay-lined depression filled with water from underground springs. It's long enough to swim laps or goof around in inner tubes. In early winter, after cold, clear weather, it freezes into thick, smooth black ice, excellent for skating in wide circles. My father liked to skate with a shovel, and when it snowed he'd make curvy paths, with a cleared rectangle for hockey games.

At first the pond was stocked with trout. I remember going to the DEC office in Canton with five-gallon buckets to collect the fish farm hatchlings. We carefully poured the little fish into the pond and waited for them to grow.

We didn't realize that others were also keeping an eye on the fish. An enterprising otter moved into the pond after the trout had gained some weight. The otter found the confined space of the pond excellent for capturing trout and efficiently ate every single one.

Another species of fish made its way up the outlet of the pond, a stream that is only inches deep for most of its route to the Grass River. Fishermen who hoped to catch trout in the pond instead pulled up whiskery bullhead.

My father admired both the otter and the bullhead for succeeding in the pond. He'd seen the otter a couple of times, when it was feasting on the trout. The sleek elegant creature had a den in the slope above the pond. When the trout were all gone, the otter moved on, but the bullhead had found a fine home, one that even served meals.

The metal garbage can by the dock has its top weighted down with big stones, to keep the raccoons away from the pellets of fish food. It's almost a ceremony—the lifting off of the heavy rocks, the clang as the lid is removed, the fishy smell of the dark green pellets as they're scooped up into a coffee can.

We make our way out onto the dock. I worry that my dad will fall in, but he is determined and stands with his legs widely braced, as if the gentle sway of the aluminum dock is actually the wildly tilting deck of a ship in a storm.

Ward, as a guest, throws in the first handful of pellets. We stare into the dark water, waiting. When nothing happens I wonder if the water temperature has gotten low enough that the bullhead are deep in the pond, suspended in cold storage until spring. But then the water ripples and wide mouths gape, gulping up the pellets that float on the surface. After they've scooped up the pellets they turn, showing their smooth gray sides, and disappear with a flick of their tails.

It's great entertainment, and the three of us watch without speaking. The pond has become an aquarium where we can watch through smoky glass the feeding habits of *Ictalurus nebulosus*.

When the fish food is all in the water and the smallest fish, patiently waiting their turn, have dared to come in and eat, we make our way back to land. My father actually lets me help him get up the slope, though my arm is tossed away as soon as he grasps his walking stick. I still haven't figured out the line between helping and annoying him; this is part of the tension between us.

Before we head back to the house, we have to play the "What kind of tree is this?" game. For years my parents tried to establish a windbreak on this side of the pond, but deer and rodents ate every tree and bush they planted. If the fenced plant did manage to survive attack, it would give up after a few winters in the fierce, bitter wind that blasts across these wide-open acres.

Finally they discovered a couple of species that could tolerate the conditions. Ward is supposed to guess what these trees are, a short row of ten-foot tall specimens in a line along the pond. One has a short, soft needle.

"Here's a hint." This is one of my dad's favorite games. "The needles won't stay on this tree all winter. It's not actually an evergreen."

Ward has no knowledge at all of plants. He shrugs.

"Tamarack!" My father almost shouts the answer. I'm glad he still remembers. He's not as sure on the other tree, a slender trunk that rises into a crown of thin branches covered in small leaves and large thorns. When he fumbles for an answer, I ask, "Is it a honey locust, Dad?"

He likes it that we're both confused. We shrug and begin the slow walk back to the house. The last of the sunlight is on the back of the barn and the massive maple tree that my father admires every day rises high above the house, its leaves still bright green, while around it lesser trees are already tinged with color.

I want to stay outside, where the cycles of life are familiar to me—the cooling of the pond, geese winging overhead, the leaves turning gold. My father's life cycle is nearing its end, and he won't be finishing in a blaze of color. He is fading in a slow decay that is painful to witness.

But here, in this open field, in the rich honey-colored light of a fall evening, we are equally in awe of the beauty of this land. I believe this delight in the natural world is at the core of my father's being, and I hope, as his body and mind continue to fail, he'll keep this joy.

We stop to rest and to admire the golden ending of the day.

THE NORTH COUNTRY
THEN AND NOW

By Gordie Little

If you accept the most liberal of definitions of "North Country," I've enjoyed all that it offers since the mid 1940s. I'm almost certain that the original Garden of Eden was located somewhere between Schroon Lake and Peasleeville. That's my story, and I'm sticking to it.

My dad was a poor preacher, and our family moved every five years or so throughout my childhood. Midway through third grade, our odyssey took us from Thornwood in Westchester County, near New York City, "upstate" to Carthage in Jefferson County. The natural beauty of the entire Thousand Islands region was not lost on me, even at that tender age. Swimming, fishing, hiking, canoeing—if it didn't cost much money, we did it all. Mother Nature served up a gorgeous setting for our family, and we took full advantage of it.

Growing up in what was then a rural community in Rockland County, my mother was a tomboy. I have seen a photograph of her doing handstands on a raft as it tumbled down the raging Ramapo River in about 1915. I was born when my mother was thirty-five, considered very "old" for childbirth in 1937. When I was about six, she taught me how to walk from Thornwood to Pleasantville on the top rails of the wooden fences along the way. Years later, at forty-nine years of age, she could run faster on stilts than I could on my feet, taking delight in jumping ditches and giggling all the while. She'd attended a Connecticut college to become a physical education instructor, until she caused damage to her knee playing field hockey, ending her career. Without surgical means to make repairs in those days, she was left with a "trick knee" that plagued her well into her eighties, but it didn't slow her down much.

I remember our first winter in Carthage. I was romping through deep snow wearing my new high-top leather boots with a jackknife pocket on the side. I fancied myself a superhero and took a flying leap off a high rock. It was a fine flight—until I hit the ground in a crumpled heap. My right leg was broken, and my screams went unheard for several hours. I spent the next eight weeks hobbling on crutches and begging my family and friends to write silly sayings on the cast.

My dad shifted from one Protestant denomination to another, and the next move brought us to a tiny community called Massena Center in St. Lawrence County. We arrived at "the Center" a few months after the earthquake of 1944 that knocked down every chimney for miles around. I have dubbed it "the little town that time forgot." Between the first time I set my limping right foot there and whenever you read this, things have changed little. I return every summer to see many of the same names on the seven dozen or so mailboxes. The 1837 iron bridge still spans the beautiful Grass River, although it has long since been closed to traffic. The adjacent fields that were once part of Tom Rickard's large farm still grow corn and grain in season. His ancestors helped to found the hamlet. The narrow, two-lane asphalt road bisects the mile-long rows of houses. Each time I return, I feel as though I've entered a time machine. I look back on my formative years there as pretty darn close to idyllic.

As children attending the 1871 two-room school next to my dad's country church, we played outside far more than most of those who are glued to their computers and TV sets these days. There were numerous games of one-o-cat, kick the can and marbles. During summer vacations, we were out the door after breakfast and were often not seen by our parents until suppertime. We built forts in the woods and made up our own games. Our toys were often things we made in our dad's garage workshop. The older boys looked after the younger ones, and there were seldom more serious emergencies than scraped knees.

We swam in the swift river without adult supervision, and as young teens, our right of passage came by swimming across—no small feat considering the current. We often camped for days at a time in the woods near the creeks that fed into the Grass River. My mother would send us off with a canvas tarp, a frying pan, a pound of lard, some matches, a hatchet and a sharp jackknife. Spearing frogs and frying their delicious legs was great fun and a good exercise in survival. We would cut small trees and boughs to make a lean-to, using our tarp over the top to keep out the rain. Sometimes it worked, and sometimes it didn't.

My mother loved North Country nature passionately; as I look back on it, she was a female Euell Gibbons. She took us on long walks, patiently explaining which wild plants and berries were edible and which were poisonous. We often came home with the powerful odor of leeks on our breath and the stain of wild berries on our lips. We learned to respect nature and to use its bountiful resources in myriad ways. Self-sufficiency was the name of the game, and we didn't want or need many adult-organized or sponsored activities to occupy our time.

Whereas many families hunker down inside during thunder and lightning storms, my mother loved to describe such events as "great adventures." As the sky was rent with a flashing light show and the rain overflowed the downspouts, Alta Grace would instruct me to put on my slicker and galoshes. With loud laughter, we would fly out the door and slosh down the middle of the country road while holding hands. "Isn't it marvelous!" she would ask, and her firm hand would allay any fears I might have had. Today, it might be considered reckless, but for me it was another lesson about nature and its many forces. As we dried off with giant, soft bath towels after our walk, she would explain the conditions that precipitated the storm, giving us a science lesson that was far better learned than any in the classroom.

Winters were as rough as or rougher than they are today, and we took full advantage of the snow and ice. Skipjacks fashioned from cordwood and barrel staves were our only means of sliding downhill, and they flew like the wind. My mother's ancient clamp-on ice skates worked just fine on frozen ponds or even on the icy roads, which had little vehicular traffic at that time.

I tacked one of my mother's white sheets to a wooden frame as a sail one day and let the brisk wind push me along at breakneck speed. My only oversight was not including a slit to see through the sheet; that trip ended with me and my sail intertwined in the ditch.

Walking or riding our bikes was the only way we got to visit our farm friends who lived as much as five miles away. We were also not averse to sticking out our thumbs to hitch a ride if our bicycle suffered a flat or a chain broke along the way. Passing motorists were almost always family friends, so there was never a threat of something untoward.

All young schoolboys and many of the girls carried a jackknife everywhere. During school recess, there were many games, including mumbly peg, and I recall no child suffering a cut from throwing the sharp implements. We also whittled, an exercise that is all but lost to the children and even adults of today. During "mud season" in spring, there were numerous games of marbles in the schoolyard and every place where a "pot" could be scooped out.

The Grass River flowed into the majestic St. Lawrence River only a few miles away, and we often walked or rode our bikes to a place called Polly's Bay for swimming and picnics. The face of the St. Lawrence and its shores was changed drastically with the completion of the St. Lawrence Seaway in the 1950s. The road from Massena Center to the big river has been closed since then.

My big brother Jim, four years my senior, and I were strong swimmers and decided at the spur of the moment we'd like to swim downriver through the swirling Little Sault Rapids that were a challenge for boaters before the Seaway obliterated them. Somehow, my dad learned of the plan. We waded in and were instantly swept away, all the time trying desperately to keep from smashing our flailing legs against the river rocks along the way. Our guardian angels worked overtime that day, and we made it through with little more than hearts beating a tattoo on the inside of our chests. As we waded ashore, we spotted our preacher dad on his knees along the shore. Apparently his supplications got to their intended destination, and he cried real tears of gratitude that his wayward sons were relatively unscathed.

We always had fishing poles and knew very well how to dig for worms. It was customary for us to melt lead with a blowtorch in our dad's shop and pour it into molds to make our own sinkers. In those days, the danger of lead in many forms was unknown.

Any money we got was earned by mowing lawns (with the old reel-type hand machines), shoveling show and doing odd jobs for neighbors. When we were old enough, we worked right along with the hired hands on Tom Rickard's farm. Tom always said that if we could do a man's work, he would pay us a man's wages. We were seasoned workers by our early teens and seemed to revel in the sweat.

My Boy Scout troop in Massena was certainly a youth highlight in my life. Learning more survival skills, camping in real tents and learning the Morse code for merit badges were all great fun. It wasn't uncommon for several Scouts to grab some grub from their mothers' larders and row out to an uninhabited St. Lawrence River island for a weekend getaway. Can you imagine parents these days allowing such adventures involving their twelve-year-old sons?

My dad was not unlike the circuit riders of yore. No single rural church could sustain a minister, so he was often charged with serving three or four of them at a time. When we lived in Massena Center, he led that church as well as Raquette River and the Indian mission church in Hogansburg.

I learned a great deal of the Native Americans' reverence for nature from various elders and even took a few lessons in the Mohawk language from the late Ray Fadden, who was a friend of the family. I played with his son John and have a treasured photograph of the two of us taken at about age ten.

I walked along the St. Regis River to places where the sweet grass grows. I drank in the wonderful odor and sat cross-legged on the floors of local homes as the senior ladies wove the grass into the most delightful baskets.

I have photographs taken in springtime with giant cakes of ice on the riverbanks, some of them causing damage to homes. To a youngster, they seemed to be five feet thick. Over the years, that image has been repeated many times as I have chosen to live very close to another river in Morrisonville, New York.

I began high school in Massena, but halfway through the year, my dad was transferred again—this time to Moira in Franklin County. The old wooden school swayed when the wind blew and was razed after centralization led to the current Brushton-Moira High School. I graduated in 1955.

I worked summers and winters for a local farmer named Dave Hiltz. He taught me the value of hard physical labor and many additional lessons that couldn't be learned in the classroom. Weather during all seasons greatly affected life on the farm and taught me humility in many ways.

As I write this and take time out to pour warm maple syrup on my wife's delicious pancakes, my reveries return to the early 1950s and spring work in a Moira-area sugar bush. Trying to keep up with my long-legged boss as he trekked through the deep snows to drill holes in the maple trees was exhausting. My job was to insert the metal taps and hang a bucket on each one. Sap was gathered by hand and dumped into a large tank drawn through the sugar bush by horses.

The heavenly smell of sap being boiled into syrup over a wood fire is as indelible in my memory as that of the Hogansburg sweet grass. And as I think back to the times I've spent traipsing around the North Country over the years, the fresh odor of pine and hemlock ranks right up near the top.

From age eight until late in high school, I always attended summer camp. The Methodist Camp Aldersgate near Lowville in the Adirondack Park was, for me, close to paradise. Swimming in Pleasant Lake, hiking on the many trails, huge nightly bonfires in the "bowl" as well as learning many arts and crafts made marvelous memories. The camp still operates to this day.

After spending a six-year period away at college, I took my first commercial radio job in Plattsburgh in 1961. Between 1955 and that time, I worked on several construction projects that allowed me to spend a lot of time outdoors. These included clearing land with a chainsaw gang near Black River for Route 81. I worked for some time on a cement crew during construction of the former Plattsburgh Air Force Base and also helped to build the Long Sault Dam and Eisenhower Lock on the St. Lawrence Seaway.

In each case, large portions of previously undeveloped land and unharnessed waterways were drastically transformed, all in the name of progress. Even as a teenager, working hard to pay for college, I suffered pangs of sadness when I saw hundreds of beautiful family farms being sold off to make way for the St. Lawrence Seaway. Many of my childhood haunts were soon lost forever. If our Native American predecessors could return to see how everything about the St. Lawrence River has changed from Massena to Ogdensburg and beyond, I wonder what their reaction would be.

Each summer, we return to our beloved St. Lawrence to camp at a place called Cole's Creek. The roadway that cuts through the camping facility is the original Route 37 from my childhood. Since the farmland was flooded and the river channel dredged for oceangoing ships, the old road breaks off on both ends of the camping area and parts of it can be seen under the water. When our children and grandchildren were small, they dubbed it "the broken road." I take great pleasure in that annual camping vacation and enjoy watching the giant ships plying the waterway. My wife, Kaye, and I walk daily along the river, trying to remember what it looked like more than fifty years ago.

As we raised our large family in the Plattsburgh area, we also spent a lot of time outside, hiking on mountain trails and walking in the woods. We used old maps to rediscover dozens of so-called ghost town sites where communities flourished over a century ago. We swam in beautiful Lake Champlain and in the Saranac River, which runs a few feet behind our Morrisonville home. We ice skated in winter wherever ice could be found and learned to ski on the local slope at nearby Beartown.

We rode our bicycles, rolled around on our roller blades and wore out many pairs of "sneakers" enjoying our North Country every chance we got. We still do. With walking, jogging and bike paths so prolific, we take full advantage. Believing in "total immersion," we love to take the less traveled paths through the woods or around another of our favorite spots—Lake Alice. The William H. Miner "million dollar dam" that creates the lake reminds us of an elephant in a flowerbed. The history of commercial blueberry-picking in that area is legendary. Not far away, a special and unique place called the Altona Flat Rock presents geology, flora and fauna that are interesting not only to us but also to professionals from around the world.

Kaye and I are bird lovers. We have had as many as fifteen feeders around our Morrisonville home and have taken great pleasure in watching them every month of the year.

As large groups of wild turkeys roost in the trees directly across our beloved Saranac River, our cameras click. We watch deer as they approach the river to drink. Click, click. We see an interesting animal we have named "Mickey the Mink" as he undulates along, looking for a mate. We thrill to the sight of an occasional bald eagle or bear cub across the meandering river. Our neighbors keep watch as well and send us frantic e-mails to say that interesting wildlife is on its way past our place. Our appreciation of the area has turned the residents into a fraternity of nature-lovers.

We have a screened deck on the back or our house, the edge of which is a scant three feet from the riverbank. For Kaye and me, sitting and listening to the constant rhythm of the river flowing by, mixed with all the sounds of nature on a spring, summer or fall day, is close to nirvana. It just doesn't get much better than that.

Coming close, though, is the beauty of nature in all seasons in the Adirondacks on regular trips to Lake Placid, Saranac Lake and Blue Mountain Lake. Although I never met the famed Adirondack hermit Noah John Rondeau, I have studied his life and have done television documentaries about this complex and fascinating character. I have also heard and shared heretofore-unknown recordings he made with friends of mine many decades ago.

I could go on. We have visited other places on earth that we've enjoyed, but we have an almost spiritual feeling about our North Country on the northern rim of New York State and long ago concluded that it truly is God's country.

Part II
The People

RAISING THE BARN

By John Berbrich

Under the blue July sky we first notice the smoke. It rises thick and black in the west, huge and threatening. We are just about to hop in the car to investigate when the fire trucks from Heuvelton come clanging by. Evidently someone's already called it in, whatever it is. We follow the trucks and don't have far to go. Around one bend in the road and over two small rises, we pull up in front of Levi's Amish farm, just three-quarters of a mile from our house. The main barn is engulfed in flames. The heat is intense; even parked alongside the road I can feel it trying to roast and crinkle my skin and blister the paint on my car.

There isn't much the fire department can do. They drag out their big hoses and spray down the nearby buildings in an attempt to keep the blaze from spreading. The barn is already a total loss. Gobs of black smoke and red flame ripple up into the air, wave after wave, distorting the blueness. Sparks shoot up. A score of people are emptying the house of its valuables and furniture, just in case the place ignites. Several men carry out a large, beautiful wood and glass hutch containing the plates and utensils. They are in a hurry and lose their grip; the hutch tips, spilling out the dishes, which shatter on the ground. Then the heavy hutch falls, smashing one of its legs. But the house doesn't catch.

Two days later, an Amish fellow stops by my house on the shore of Mud Lake. He doesn't ask, but rather suggests, that they could use a little help up at Levi's place the next day and that I should bring my chainsaw.

I show up the next morning around eight o'clock, with my twenty-inch chainsaw, a can of oil-gas mixture, a container of engine oil and two freshly sharpened chains. Another "Englisch" man is there, a guy named Bill, also with a chainsaw. With us are a dozen or so Amish men of varying ages, all clad in plain dark blue trousers, long-sleeved shirts, hats and black boots. I don't see Levi.

An Amish man named Dennis explains the plan. Levi's burly uncle Ben lives at the farm next door. Ben also operates a sawmill on his property. He and Levi have drawn up plans for a new barn. Ben has given Dennis a list of the dimensions of all the wood that he will need for lumber. Bill and I, along with our chainsaws and the Amish men, are to head out into the deep woods behind the pasture on horse-drawn wagons.

So we load up. The horses pull the wagons along the roadside and then turn off onto a path through a field. Out here I feel that I am entering new territory. I can smell the hot fragrance of the vegetation and watch the wagon's big iron wheels turning. We splash through a small creek and then enter the cool shadows of the woods. At this point, the wagons stop and we disembark. From here we continue on foot along a path, carrying our gear, heading deeper and deeper into the woods.

Bill and a few of the Amish go on ahead, sawing down and limbing suitable trees as they go. They soon are out of sight, although I still can hear the periodic snarl of Bill's chainsaw. Dennis and I follow behind. Each time we come to a downed tree, Dennis consults Ben's list, attached to a clipboard. Dennis measures each tree for total length and breadth, determining what lengths he needs for each. This is where I come in, my chainsaw roaring to life, slicing the trunk at the appropriate spots. After usually two or three cuts, Dennis and I roll the logs apart and he writes with a heavy red marker on the end, designating exactly what pieces of lumber this is designed for.

Dennis runs his own sawmill and knows something about lumber, and after a while it becomes obvious to me that he doesn't approve of Ben's calculations. He grumbles, "Now why does he want...?" while doing some figuring with a pencil and paper. But even while muttering and shaking his head, Dennis complies with Ben's requests.

Some of the other Amish guys lead the horses into the woods. They secure the fallen trees with heavy chains, which are then fastened around the necks of these beautiful work animals. The horses drag the logs along the path and out into the pasture, where the men manage to load them onto the wagons and cart them over to the sawmill. It's quite an operation we have going. I notice that the Amish never clear-cut anything, unless perhaps they are converting woodland into farmland. I watch the great, muscular horses work and then imagine noisy, heavy machines ripping and bulldozing. Large balls of hay-brown poop tumble from a horse's rear; "road apples," the Amish call them with a grin.

We take periodic short breaks, giving Dennis and me a chance to talk. I ask him why it's okay for the Amish to use diesel engines to power their sawmills but not okay for them to use chainsaws. He looks pretty thoughtful at that one and takes his time answering. He finally says that he doesn't really know the answer, that both are internal combustion engines and that ultimately the decision rests with the local bishop.

I love to listen to these men say the word *Englisch*, their usual designation for non-Amish folks. The *sh* sound is pronounced in a thicker way, giving the word a lot more heft. I also find out from Dennis that he's very interested in history, although he doesn't elaborate on this. I wonder why all these Amish fellows have long wild hair and beards, but not one grows a mustache. This seems a bit personal, so I don't ask about it.

Throughout the morning and the afternoon we work. I'm covered with sawdust and sweat. Dennis and I share water from a plastic milk container. Toward the end of the afternoon everyone has had enough. The horses have one more log to drag out. The chain is secured, and an Amish fellow named Johnnie is leading the horses, sort of pulling them along on a slight run. Johnnie has red hair and a red beard. Bill, the other Englisch, says in a loud voice, "Those horses couldn't make it without Johnnie pulling them along," and everyone laughs.

We load up in the wagons. I am exhausted. We bump our way back across the field, returning to the glare of summer heat. Up by the house I climb off, taking my trusty chainsaw and gear with me. The barn is a collapsed, black, smoking wreck. I toss my things in the car. The Amish are driving the wagons over to Ben's sawmill next door to drop off the logs; my day is done, but theirs isn't. They all need to get back to their own farms, pounding in fence posts and milking cows by hand.

The barn smokes and smolders for two weeks. Persistent westerly winds bring the stench of charred wood and burned cows directly to my house. But then within a week the land is cleared and the new barn erected. The frame goes up on a rainy day, scores of blue-clad Amish raising the walls. My wife is there, quilting with the Amish women and helping to prepare food for everyone. Driving by, I'm kind of pleased that I was able to help out and to know that those logs I cut with my own chainsaw were actually helping to hold that new structure together. Eventually, Dennis visits and admires my home library, particularly my history books.

—◦◦◦—

Several years have passed. We've moved away from Mud Lake. Uncle Ben is dead. Levi and his family have moved to Minnesota. And Dennis, well, he's been shunned by the Amish community for displaying an unacceptable interest in computer technology. But that barn, in sunshine, wind, snow, ice and rain, still stands tall.

WHERE THE LOCALS EAT

By Varick Chittenden

It's mid-morning, and I'm on my way from Canton to Utica. I've taken the back roads—through DeGrasse, Fine, Harrisville and Croghan—and arrive in Lowville, just in time for a late breakfast.

After passing through the picturesque village heading south, I come to a Y in the road. From there, I can take Route 12 to Utica or, bearing right, follow 26 toward Rome. At that intersection is my destination of the moment, Lloyd's of Lowville, about as traditional a hometown diner as you can find. The long, low structure, with a semi-quonset roof and fake stone siding, is topped by a bright neon sign out of the 1950s.

Several vehicles populate the small parking lot—local cars and pickup trucks, with a motorcycle or two. For farmers who've finished their morning chores and workers from the Kraft plant—the world's largest producer of cream cheese—and the AMF bowling pin factory across the street, this is coffee break time, so the diner is bustling with activity and chatter. Lloyd's is homemade, unlike one of those factory-built iconic diner cars of the early twentieth century, with glistening stainless steel everywhere. Here the interior is well-worn wood and Formica and vinyl.

I grab a seat in the only available booth and am quickly met by a friendly waitress—Sue, according to her nametag. She offers coffee and, since I'm an obvious outsider, a menu. Breakfasts are available from early morning until closing in the evening, but I scan the menu for other options—lots of good diner fare. At home, I'm not much of a breakfast eater, but on the road, I look for places like Lloyd's. I find a favorite—corned beef hash—so when Sue comes back I order it with two poached eggs and homemade whole-wheat toast.

Sharon, the short-order cook and one of several longtime Lloyd's employees, tends to her business behind the long counter but keeps up with the locals' banter. The police chief occupies a stool at the counter, eating his breakfast and joking with a couple of men about some nameless miscreants who've been at it again overnight. An older woman in the booth next to me talks to the waitress, who has delivered her doughnut; it's clear she now lives alone and comes to the diner nearly every day, for food and company.

I'm next up. Sue delivers my meal without fanfare. The hash has been browned crisp on the grill, the eggs are on top of the hash—just as I ordered—and the thick slices of toast are golden brown and buttered just right. Perfect! She brings the pot of steaming coffee back to offer a refill in my heavy, blue-and-white ceramic mug that declares on one side "Lloyd's of Lowville" and, on the other, "A Landmark Diner." While clearly not a place that has much interest in, or need for, marketing, it recognizes its history and its importance to the community. I've been told that the restaurant was established in 1939 and was owned for many years by Lloyd Rasmussen, also its chief cook and bottle washer, thus its name. Very little has changed since.

As I enjoy my meal—and the surroundings—I contemplate a complete blowout of a sensible day of eating. A half dozen pies in a glass case behind the counter have been capturing my attention since I sat down, and I'm tempted. Better judgment prevails: I order a piece of apple pie to take out. I simply can't go to Lloyd's and leave without it. By that time, the coffee break crowd is leaving, the cooks are preparing for the noon rush for lunch and I have to be on my way. I take my check to the counter where Sue makes change, grab the Styrofoam box with a sizeable wedge of pie and head for the road.

—⚬⚬⚬—

I like to eat, and I like to cook. While I don't profess to be very good at either one, I find food intriguing and the customs and traditions that people have developed around food fascinating. As remote as we are from major cities where style is important and trends are often set, the North Country has managed to produce several fine restaurants and locally-celebrated chefs. If you're a self-professed foodie, these are the places you may find most attractive. They're especially right for more elaborate entertaining, closing a business deal or a romantic date night. The chefs experiment with different ingredients and cooking techniques; the setting for dining is carefully planned; and the service is choreographed to a T. Don't get me wrong: I enjoy those experiences. As a folklorist, though, I appreciate the stuff of everyday life, especially the traditions that help to identify a community of like-minded people and have survived through the years.

When it comes to food, then, I look for places where the locals eat. Today, that can mean McDonald's, Burger King, Subway or Pizza Hut, but that's fast food, quick service, takeout or drive-through. They're cookie-cutter look-alikes, designed and operated with a corporate mentality and without much personality.

For me, "where the locals eat" means where people gather not only for homestyle food they can count on but also for good talk, for meeting friends and for feeling like part of a place. Unlike the McDonald's that was ironically built right next door a few years ago, Lloyd's is like that, well-established and vital to life in the community. While I was there, Sue told me, "We have regulars that sit in the same booth every single day and order the same meal every single day. They'll wait in the parking lot in the morning for us to open the door. We have mostly local people, in the summer time some travelers, of course. But, if we didn't have our locals, we wouldn't have anything at all. We love our locals."

Restaurants have a very high failure rate. A recent industry study shows that one of every four closes within a year of opening, about 60 percent within three years. It's a tough business, especially for small independent operators who have a dream but little experience. I like to try new ones, but I'm especially partial to those that have been around a long time. They have a loyal following and lots of character (and, usually, lots of characters!). They've become fixtures in their communities and, quite often, favorite spots for visitors traveling through. Lloyd's is one of those places. Others in the North Country stand out for me as well.

———

The Cascade Inn perches on the western bank of the Grasse River, at the intersection of routes 11 and 68 in Canton, where many travelers funnel into the village from the south and west. Named for its view of the beautiful waterfall in the river below, it was opened by Gary and Winnie Barcomb in 1958, when they moved the vintage Miss Canton Diner from a downtown block. In 1961, they added a twenty-room motel, still a popular place for traveling salesmen and construction workers, as well as families on a budget.

Gary was killed in an auto accident in 1963; the diner burned in 1965. Unbowed by these tragedies, Winnie—who later married Floyd Gushea— rebuilt the restaurant on-site, with a diner-like lunch counter and booths and an attached dining room with a cocktail lounge below. She has been there ever since, the doyenne of the diner crowd and overseer of the books.

The Cascade has also had a regular following of local people from the beginning. The restaurant opens at 6:00 a.m. daily (except Monday, plus a few weeks in January and February) and stays open until 10:00 at night, 9:00 on Sunday. Like many a good diner, the Cascade serves breakfast all day long. Some local men arrive very early, for their first coffee of the day and a chance to read their papers. Winnie says that certain people have their spots: attorney John Elmer always sits at the first table in the dining room; businessman Roger Morgan favors the last table in the diner proper; and octogenarian "Tunk" Bisnett can be found almost daily on a stool at the end of the counter, where he can see everything and everyone.

The highlight of the day at the Cascade for many locals is mid-morning. "The Coffee Boys," as Winnie calls them, is a group of up to fourteen men who gather every weekday at 10:00 in the dining room for coffee and talk. Begun in 1954 at Ralph's up the street, the cast of characters has changed since, but little else. Charter member Frank White, a canoeist and retired florist in his nineties, still joins landscaper Bill Locy, retired restaurateur Ted Lawrence, retired engineering professor Otis Van Horne, accountant Brian Staples and bank president Dave Swanson. Morning waitress Connie Chase, a Cascade veteran of twenty-five years, is caretaker for the group nearly every day. She has them trained to pay one check, a condition that has prompted an elaborate daily ritual for deciding who gets that honor. Another waitress told me, "they discuss anything and everything" and that "it sometimes gets pretty hectic in there."

Not to be outdone, a smaller group of women—"The Coffee Girls"—meets a couple of mornings each week at 9:00, for breakfast or coffee. They often celebrate birthdays or special occasions at their favorite table in the dining room.

The Cascade menu has a dazzling number of choices for breakfast, lunch or dinner. Gloria Jennings, who has waited tables in Canton for forty-one years, says of the Cascade, "You name it, we've got it!" One recent day, the lunch specials included a pulled pork barbecue sandwich with baked beans and cole slaw or a Glazier's hot dog, a North Country favorite. Winnie proudly declares that all the baking—bread, rolls, cakes, doughnuts and pies—is done on the premises daily. She adds, "We roast the turkey breasts, make gravies, everything from scratch."

As for crowd favorites, Gloria says Cascade omelets are the best and that Roxy Coffey, Winnie's daughter and a breakfast cook, is famous for hers. Other specialties are Friday night fish fries and Saturday night prime rib, each with a following of regulars. For me, the winners are macaroni and cheese—one of my personal tests of diner food—on Fridays and any of their pies.

My favorite recollection of this Canton institution is of a time when it was, literally, a beacon in a storm—the infamous Ice Storm of 1998. While much of the region was without electricity for well over a week, the Cascade stayed open through it all. Winnie's son Gary, who does a variety of necessary tasks, was cooking at the time. He told me, "We cook with natural gas—even our coffee maker uses gas—so we were OK. I laugh to think of it now, but for a few days I made whatever I could in the kitchen with a flashlight attached to my hat. We never closed, stayed open 24/7 for at least a week. If people could pay, they did. If they couldn't, that was OK, too." After several days of cold cereal and closed roads, we heard that the Cascade was open. With dreams of a hot meal and real people for company, we made our way there. What a welcome sight. Breakfast is always good there, but that time it was perfect!

⋘⋙

Most any time of day or night, if I'm in Ogdensburg and I'm hungry, I think of Phillips Diner. It's been a downtown fixture there as long as I can remember, and then some. While on a recent visit to "the Burg," I stopped in.

Once inside its red, white and blue exterior, my eyes scan, from left to right, the red Formica counter with about eight high-back swivel bar stools, then a row of snug booths and, finally, a row of tables with picture-window views of Ford Street and historic city hall. There's not much room to spare. The counter area alone was the original 1930 diner, first called the Theater Dining Car, because the Strand Theater stood next door. The diner quickly became a favorite place to eat before and after the latest movies. As the diner prospered, enough seats were eventually added to accommodate as many as seventy. The black-and-white vinyl floor tiles in a checkerboard design, honey-color stained beadboard on the walls and ceiling and padded vinyl booth seats seem to say, "Come on in. Seat yourself. Feel right at home."

I thought I'd avoid the lunch rush by arriving about 1:30 on a Thursday afternoon in January. Not so. I spot only one empty table very near the back and head for it, a perfect place to watch and listen. One of the waitresses comes right up and hands me a menu, which includes a one-page description of the diner's history. I'll get to that later. In a minute, she's back—I later find out her name is Tabitha—and I order a hot meatloaf sandwich, fries ("with brown gravy") and a Pepsi. How diner-like is that? She takes off on a run, and that's the way she works all the time I'm there—friendly, quick, always in motion, all over the room.

I keep a menu to study the diner's story. It says, in part, that Russell, Ollie and son Bud Phillips purchased the diner in 1948 and opened as Phillips Diner. They owned and operated it until 1970, when their son-in-law, Joe Rish, took over. After the diner suffered extensive damage when a fire destroyed the theater next door, Joe decided to repair it and bought it from Bud Phillips in 1973. Joe's daughter Judy Ashley and her husband, Don, purchased it in 1994 and have continued since.

Before I know it, the food arrives, and I'm happy. After a generous wedge of lemon meringue pie and coffee, I get to meet Judy. A very pleasant middle-aged woman, it's clear that she's proud of the diner and her family's long history with it. She tells me, "I'm very lucky that it has stayed around as it has. When my father passed away, I hesitated about taking it on because it was family and it was my grandparents'. Were we going to be able to make it? The staff and the customers are why we're still here. They are very loyal, and we try not to change things. That's a big part of it."

This day, the lunch crowd is pretty much of Social Security vintage. Judy describes the two couples sharing a booth across from me as "real regulars," and there are many others like them. They come there nearly every day for lunch. She says, "There are people that come in here still on Sunday mornings that were here when I was a little girl. And I'm in my fifties." She adds, though, that the crowd changes all day and all week; business owners and laborers come in for breakfast, teenagers love to stop in after school and on weekend nights (they're open until 3:00 a.m. on Fridays and Saturdays, open again at 5:00 a.m.), it's yet another crowd. Judy laughs, "It's amazing what people eat, especially in the wee hours of the morning, after a couple of cocktails. I'm amazed at what they'll order. And it's crazy in here, packed, amazing."

Several hand-painted wooden signs that hang above the lunch counter attract my attention. One advertises the "Sunrise Special" with eggs, toast, home fries and coffee, another a "Pile 'em High Pancake Special"—breakfast is served all day and night—and a third "The Original Deluxe Bacon Cheeseburger." I ask Judy about a fourth sign, "Businessman Special/Open Steak/Served w/ French Fries Toss Salad/ $11.25." It's the only steak they serve, a fourteen-ounce rib-eye, hand-cut by the Phillips cooks. She says these specials and the signs have been around as long as she can remember. Over the years, they've been repainted only to clean them up or change the prices.

Two other items are popular customer choices as well: home fries and—remember it?—brown gravy. Judy says, "I have recipes in a book that we hide. They were my grandfather's and my father's that were passed on." She tells me what's special about their home fries—they are first boiled, then baked and "then we put them on the grill before they hit your plate." I think she left out a secret ingredient or two! And the gravy (made from the juices of many pounds of beef roasted in the Phillips kitchen each week) is a customer favorite. "Gravy on the French fries, that's a huge thing here. Same recipe as thirty years ago."

When Tabitha brings the check to my table, I notice that she's wearing a Phillips Diner t-shirt with a slogan in a colorful design on the back: "Our Food is So Good You'd Think We Kidnapped Your Mother!" I like that. By now, the crowd has thinned out a little, and she's the only waitress in the place. Judy tells me, "She's fabulous. She's been here seven years, started as a teenager. The only one in here right now, and she's handling the whole building by herself. That's the kind of staff we have here."

As I get ready to leave, she adds, "I think everybody in the family worked here. And I think everybody in Ogdensburg has worked here in one position or another, either as a waitress, a dishwasher, a cook, or…I think everybody in Ogdensburg has some kind of ties to the diner. This is sixty-five years this year. And we really haven't changed a lot."

———⟨ø∩ø⟩———

When Longway's Diner was built in 1966, it was at the end of Interstate 81. It was as far north as you could go on a four-lane highway coming from Syracuse and points south. And it was the beginning of busy traffic, especially for big rigs hauling all kinds of goods into or out of the North Country. Businessman Doug Longway saw a need he could fill, and an opportunity, so he built a diner as well as a truck stop near Exit 48. Little did he likely realize it at the time, but he'd also built a landmark for all kinds of travelers, any time of day or night, in all kinds of weather, including the North Country's infamous, blinding Lake Effect blizzards.

Larry Longway, Doug's son, now says with a chuckle, "People might think so, but we have never been a family of cooks." He adds that the diner was always one of several kinds of businesses they have owned and that several people have leased it from the family-owned corporation over the years. Leon Walts, the current manager, has worked for the Longways for twenty years and "is the food guy." Longway says that, until the 1990s, "90 percent of the business was truckers and workers from the local mills, mostly paper mills." He adds that, at its busiest, the truck stop parking lot was bumper-to-bumper eighteen-wheelers, with license plates from as many places as you could imagine in the United States and Canada. When the mills began to close down, the Longways sold the truck stop, and the diner's business became more and more local retirees and army personnel from nearby Fort Drum.

Longway's Diner has always been open 24/7—it has never closed since it opened forty-seven years ago. Despite the change in clientele over the years, it still caters to hungry people with big appetites. Besides more realistic choices, the breakfast menu features a "Trucker Breakfast" with a ten-ounce top round steak, two eggs, home fries and toast; stacks of pancakes (your choice of plain, blueberry, strawberry or chocolate chip); and the "Garbage Omelette," a concoction of six eggs, sausage patties, bacon, ham, tomato, onion, green peppers, mushrooms, spinach, and broccoli.

Longway's is one of the few local diners that still has the grill directly behind the counter, so visitors can watch the food being prepared before their eyes. That has always been a fascination for me and, obviously, for others as well. Father Dominic Grassi, a Chicago priest who finds spirituality in all kinds of common human experiences, wrote a short story in 1999, which he called "Ode to a Short Order Cook." In it, he describes a memory from his boyhood: "I was mesmerized by the energy and economy of motion as this cook worked the grill, the toasters, the burners, the coolers. No matter how busy he was, he displayed this intensity and a sense of confident organization. He was in control at all times. To a klutzy ten-year-old, he was a marvel to watch."

To an envious folklorist, watching Lori Woodard at the Longway's grill gets some of the same reactions from me. Stopping at the diner about 11:30 on a Sunday morning, I'm lucky to get a stool at the counter so I can see her in action. The place is packed, and the orders are coming in fast and furiously: pancakes, oatmeal, French toast, biscuits and gravy, cinnamon rolls, bagels, you name it. The most popular, it seems, is the "Breakfast Special #1": two eggs (any way you want), two slices of bacon, two links of sausage, one pancake, home fries and toast (for $7.79!). That would be a true test for a short-order cook, and Lori certainly seems up for it. She works methodically, never seeming to get flustered. She breaks eggs, flips pancakes, turns bacon, sausages and home fries, butters toast, all in one continuing movement, over and over again. Poetry in motion, I'd call it; all in a day's work is what she'd say. On one short break in the action, I find out that Lori has been at Longway's for twenty-six years, the only place she's ever worked. She cooks a couple days a week; the rest of the time she's a waitress and assistant manager.

People in their Sunday best arrive after church, others in sports clothes before the football or basketball game begins on TV. Young men and women in camo gear come in when the shift is over at Fort Drum; others, with small children in tow, wait for an empty seat. I get up to go, completely satiated and ready for my own over-the-highway road trip.

—◦◦◦—

If you've never been to the Crystal Restaurant on Public Square in Watertown, plan a visit soon. As an old-fashioned downtown eatery, it's as classic as they come in the North Country. Whether you're looking for eggs over easy for breakfast or a quick tuna salad sandwich for lunch, "the Crystal" is the place to go in Watertown and has been since the Dephtereos family took over in the early 1940s. From the classic gilded signs on the exterior windows to the pressed tin ceiling, mosaic tile floor and dark wood booths that line the perimeter, this always-busy restaurant is a highlight of the once-bustling Public Square.

The interior is really like a movie set, where you might easily expect to see Viggo Mortensen or Richard Grieco, both hometown boys, consuming their generous helpings of pancakes or burgers and fries, surrounded by cameras and crew. More commonly, you will find lawyers in business suits at one table, a family with young children at the next and senior citizens lounging with their coffee mugs at yet another, conversation flowing freely among them. The Crystal boasts one of the last stand-up bars in the country and some of the cheapest prices for food. The menu is classic, too, comfort food at its best, with all the standards you'd expect. Meatloaf, ham steak, liver and onions, chili, cole slaw, rice pudding—you know what I mean.

The Crystal is one of those places that instills loyalty in its owners, its staff and its customers. Peter Dephtereos, third-generation and the current owner, grew up in the business. He has an MBA from Syracuse University, but you can find him most any day in the kitchen, cooking if he's needed, but also making certain that the restaurant preserves its well-deserved reputation. Several Crystal waitresses have been there for some time, too, but none compares with Marion. She was full-time for over forty years until her recent retirement, and she still returns from her winter home in Florida to work a few hours a week each summer. Customers who go way back swap favorite stories with Marion about Peter's Uncle Leo, the genial host who welcomed everyone and made sure that they were treated right for many years. Helen Mattraw has been a "regular" since she was six years old, more than eighty years ago.

From Thanksgiving through New Year's, late afternoons and early evenings at the Crystal are party time. For longer than Peter can remember, the main attraction has been Tom & Jerrys, a hearty punch served warm in mugs from an antique ceramic bowl that once perched on the bar in the long-gone historic Hotel Woodruff on the Square. Ingredients for a "T&J" include a frothy egg batter and a shot each of brandy and rum, topped with cinnamon and nutmeg. A few unidentified ingredients are still a family secret.

By the week before Christmas, the crowd starts gathering around four o'clock, as dusk begins to descend. By six o'clock one day, a friend and I can hardly find a place to stand. Couples and small groups come in from the cold to sample the drink and have fun in a friendly atmosphere. Peter and his staff constantly run in from the kitchen with fresh batches of punch. While we're waiting for a refill, watching the bartender prepare the mugs and pour and decorate the drinks is part of the entertainment. Tom & Jerrys at the Crystal have become such a Watertown tradition that some call it a "must do" at least once each year. You should try it.

—◁◦◦◦▷—

When the St. Lawrence Seaway construction project was in full swing in the early 1950s, "Theresa Bear" Lazore took in construction workers as boarders in her St. Regis Indian Reservation home and served them evening meals. Because she was on the busy state highway, she also put in a couple of gas pumps, along with a snack bar and souvenir shop for the tourist trade. There she featured her own leatherwork, dolls and traditional Mohawk beadwork, as well as the celebrated sweet grass "fancy baskets" of other women of the reservation in her Bear's Den Trading Post.

Theresa's son Eli Tarbell and his wife, Gretchen, now operate the trading post at Akwesasne, a real fixture along Route 37 east of Massena. The Tarbells remain close to their family roots with the business now into its fourth generation. Before they had such a big operation, Eli taught school at nearby Salmon River Central, where many Mohawk children have gone over the years. Typical of many Mohawk men, he also worked on high steel construction projects all over the Northeast. With no previous restaurant experience, Gretchen was the short-order cook when they opened the establishment in 1983.

It's a complex, sophisticated business today, a far cry from the way it was at the beginning. There are multiple gas pumps, a convenience store, car wash, tobacco shop, native gift shop and the Bear's Den Restaurant, all doing a thriving business. While it's popular with area families, the restaurant is also a busy stop for truckers and passersby. The Mohawk Bingo Palace is a short distance west and the Mohawk Casino about the same to the east. Gas and cigarettes at bargain prices are also a big attraction to "the rez," so there are plenty of opportunities up and down the highway to stock up.

Because I go to Akwesasne fairly often to visit the museum or any number of artists, I like to stop there for lunch. It's much more pleasant these days, with good non-smoking rooms available. It's interesting too because of the mix of customers. You often see men with coal-black hair in single long braids down their backs, sometimes to the waist. Women and children—and sometimes men—may be dressed in colorful traditional ribbon shirts. You may be surrounded with people quietly conversing in Mohawk, with a cadence that's fascinating to English ears. It may be pretty obvious to the regulars that you are a visitor to town.

The breakfast menu presents choices I could find elsewhere: omelets, pancakes, home fries. But I also see eggs Benedict, breakfast quesadillas and strawberry-stuffed French toast, perhaps reflecting the influence of Eli and Gretchen's daughter Christy. A graduate of the culinary arts program at Johnson and Wales, she's now in the business.

At lunchtime, there are Grizzly Burgers and Kodiak Wraps, but I go for the Mohawk Indian Corn Soup. The menu describes it as "a traditional favorite among our locals and a must try for tourists looking for an authentic Mohawk dish! Our recipe secrets make it a homemade special." Since it's a secret, I have to guess what's in it—white hulled corn (the kind a few regional gardeners still raise, braid, dry and process by leaching the hulls in wood ashes), kidney beans and winter squash (the familiar Three Sisters of Iroquois legend), a light broth (I think chicken), potatoes, carrots and salt and pepper to taste. A bowl served hot with a side order of traditional fry bread makes a really good stick-to-your-ribs meal.

I'm told that, as a special, the cooks at Bear's Den occasionally make "Indian hash," a robust mixture of ground beef, sausage, potatoes, onion and poultry seasoning (or some variation). This has long been a traditional dish for Mohawk wedding feasts, and Gretchen tells me that it sells out fast when they make it. I've never been lucky enough to be there in time. That's an advantage of being a local!

—◈—

If it's summertime and I'm anywhere near Plattsburgh, I have to make a run to Clare & Carl's. Located on the south side of town, near the old airbase, this simple clapboard-and-glass brick roadside stand has been near and dear to the hearts of townsfolk and travelers alike since it was built by Carl and Clare Warne in 1942. It's actually an architectural wonder that it's still standing at all, as each year it seems to slowly sink a little more into the ground. But not for lack of business; its appearance only adds to its charm. Whenever I go, the place is buzzing. The parking lot is usually full; car hops dash around taking orders and returning with trays to clamp on customers' car windows. It's a small-town version of Mel's Drive-In that stayed around. Some choose to go inside, where there's a small U-shaped counter with a few padded stools and an opportunity to see the cooks in action.

Clare & Carl's is the granddaddy of local "michigan" stands. Much has been written and said about hot dogs in America, and there seems to be an endless variety of ways to serve them. In the Champlain Valley, since the 1920s there is only one way: the michigan, the local chili dog, named for a state hundreds of miles from northern New York. While the franks and the sauces may vary somewhat from stand to stand in the area, on a visit to town a few years ago the celebrated food adventurers Jane and Michael Stern wrote of Clare & Carl's: "[It] presents its michigans in an ineffably tender bun that is similar to the traditional Northeast split-top but thicker at the bottom and closed on both ends, forming a trough to contain the sloppy topping. The chili is thick with minced meat, kaleidoscopically spiced, not at all sweet, and just barely hot." To that, I would add the Warnes' requisite swipe of yellow mustard and chopped onions, "on top" or "buried." The Sterns' conclusion: "It is intriguing and addictive."

Like most local legends, the story of "michigans" coming to Plattsburgh has many variations. Terry and Brian Spiegel—the current stewards of Clare & Carl's since Terry inherited it from her first husband, a nephew of the Warnes—like the version published in the old *Plattsburgh Daily Press*. That credits Eula Otis, a short-order cook from Michigan who worked there, with often saying, "I'm from Michigan. Would you like to try one of our chili dogs?" Eventually she became known by the name of her native state. Her sauce recipe, and her nickname, seemed to stick. Years later, it's become so popular that several other stands around town have loyal followings as well, among them McSweeney's, Ronnie's and Gus's Red Hots. I'm told that michigans are even on the menu in the cafeteria at Plattsburgh's CVPH Medical Center.

While michigans are the big draw at Clare & Carl's, it also serves a really good sandwich with deep-fried whitefish on a soft roll, hamburgers or cheeseburgers made the old-fashioned way while you wait and onion rings that are fresh-cut and deep-fried. You might not want to go for a cholesterol test right after lunch here, but you surely will remember it and long to go back.

<hr />

There's not much evident ethnic diversity in the North Country these days or authentic traditional ethnic food. Canton and Potsdam, college towns, have seen restaurants for Chinese, Tex-Mex, Indian, Thai, Moroccan, Latino and Jamaican food come and, quite often, go. Although Shine and Beverly Sabad retired and sold their family restaurant in Norfolk a few years ago, the new owners continue to serve Hungarian dishes like chicken paprikash, cabbage rolls and handmade cabbage noodles. In their nineteenth-century Lake Clear Lodge in the northern Adirondacks, Cathy and Ernest Hohmeyer offer scores of European beers and wines and a selection of schnitzels, sauerbraten and strudels from his German family cookbook. And in Watertown, which claims by far the greatest diversity of cultures in the North Country today thanks largely to its proximity to Fort Drum, there's the Apollo Restaurant tucked into a shopping mall, still offering up favorites of the Greek community like moussaka, stuffed grape leaves and baklava.

One exception is Italian; that you find everywhere. I have fond memories of trips to Tardelli's in Potsdam for pizza or pasta as a teenager, to Zasa's in Canton in my college days and to the Roma in Gouverneur as a young teacher there. Many years later there's still Sergi's in Canton and Potsdam, Sansone's in Malone, the Belvedere in Saranac Lake, Cavallario's in Alexandria Bay, Art's Jug in Watertown and Violi's in Massena. Sadly, the Roma, Zasa's and Tardelli's are gone now, but the others are still alive and well, none more so than Arnie's Restaurant in Plattsburgh.

After an enthusiastic recommendation from a friend who grew up there, I made my first trip to Arnie's recently. As I parked on Margaret Street in downtown Plattsburgh and headed for the center of the block, I spotted a colorful neon sign overhead, declaring "Arnie's Restaurant, Bar, Italian and American." Arnie Pavone, the family patriarch, would later proudly tell me that he recently had to fight local ordinances to keep that sign there. Officials relented after they decided that it was an important historical artifact.

A roomy bar is on the main floor, a favorite after-work stop and a great place to wait for a table and catch up on local news. The restaurant is up a narrow set of stairs, where it's been since the Pavones opened there in 1956. For years they also ran a shoe repair and model train shop on the first floor, in the best tradition of North Country eclecticism. From my table near the top of the stairs, I can spot some framed prints of the Italian countryside, old family portraits and a collection of autographed photos of sports stars and other celebrities who have eaten there in the past. Arnie and I reminisce about one, Carmen Basilio, the world champion welterweight boxer from the 1950s, who was a boyhood hero of mine.

The business began in 1951, when Arnie and his wife, Betty, started out on Charlotte Street a few blocks away, in the old Italian neighborhood. For income during World War II, Arnie's mother, Natalina, had run a "spaghetti house" in one room of the family home where, as he tells it, she served army boys from the local base who came into town on payday. Her reputation as a good cook soon spread, and she often cooked for weddings or other special events in a hall in town. Arnie had started out as a bartender down the street, so when the tavern came up for sale, he decided that it would be a better location for their restaurant, and it has been there since.

Natalina—and her recipes—came to America from Ascoli Piceno on the central west coast of Italy. Much-prized by the family, those recipes have remained the mainstay of the menu to this day. Minestrone soup and antipasto salads accompany pasta dishes like lasagna, manicotti and fettuccine Alfredo, as well as veal scallopini, eggplant parmigiana or chicken cacciatora. At the public's request, pizza was added in later years and became popular, but it was never Natalina's favorite. Since her time, they haven't tinkered with her recipes or tried to become "fine dining," since they and their customers have been perfectly happy as they were. Pork chops, shrimp platters, strip steaks, ham and lobster appear on the menu, but most regulars come for authentic Italian comfort food, Arnie's style. I choose a small antipasto salad and a perpetual favorite of mine, baked lasagna. It comes in a generous portion, with a delightful red sauce, three cheeses and plenty of meat, well worth my two-hour trip from home.

The online travel guide TripAdvisor encourages people to add their reviews of food and lodging, so you can see what customers really think. Among the postings about Arnie's is one by Phil of Connecticut: "My first visit was in 1956, when the only real Italian food you could get in the North Country was in your own kitchen. We couldn't afford to go [out] often so it was a real treat to go to Arnie's. I don't live in town anymore but visit for Thanksgiving and always make a reservation at Arnie's for Friday night…and the place is always packed. That speaks volumes as to the consistency and quality of your dining experience at Arnie's."

The food is predictable and good, but according to Glenn, one of three sons who have stayed in the business, many customers still come because of Arnie himself. Now an energetic and healthy-looking eighty-seven, he still comes in every day, runs the front office, writes the checks and, most of all, welcomes his guests as though they are family. Glenn says, "The first thing they ask is 'Where's Arnie?' It pleases him that some children come in with grandparents who he served as kids a long time ago. Who else can say that?"

—◆◆◆—

Culinary tourism is experiencing the food of the country, region or area and is now considered a vital component of the tourism experience. The North Country is not the usual culinary tourist's first-choice destination. Santa Fe is; New Orleans is. Places like that, in folklorists' or anthropologists' terms, are cultural hearths, where a specific culture, including its food choices, evolves, often a mix of a dominant ethnic heritage and regional growing conditions. Local foods and food customs can contribute a lot to the unique identity of a city or a whole region and give it great appeal to visitors.

Aside from church suppers, firemen's fish fries or chicken barbecues, it's the diners and small family restaurants that dominate North Country choices for eating out. Besides those described above, of course, there are many other notable places to eat in the vast North Country that are popular in their vicinities. Using my own criteria for a landmark eatery—an appealing ambience, a great place for community gatherings, authentic food choices and longevity of service—limits the list significantly.

Several stand out in my mind. Going west to east, there's the Koffee Kove in Clayton with a casual mix of local regulars and tourists and its booths made from the sternboards of local river boats. There's Shultz's Family Restaurant in Croghan (when Norm Shultz owned it, he called it Shultz's Fastidious Foods), with the big woodstove in the center of the dining room for cold winter days; Guy's Restaurant & Drive-in east of Massena, built in the early 1950s to serve three shifts of St. Lawrence Seaway construction workers; and Jumbo's Dinette (one of my favorite oxymorons), still in downtown Gouverneur, but with an all-new look in recent years.

Travelers on Route 11 between Richville and Dekalb Junction recognize the Silver Leaf Diner—so named in the 1950s by the original owner for a silver leaf maple tree in the yard, long gone now. Today the diner is owned by Loretta Thayer, famous for her pies and North Country favorites like chicken and biscuits, roast pork and Friday fish fries. In April, people line up for bullheads, the catfish-like seasonal standard, caught expressly for the diner by a local fisherman. At Eben's Hearth in Potsdam, you'll find college students and their families in season and a lively sports bar year-round, especially in college hockey season, with pub food and specialty sandwiches named for citizens prominent in Potsdam's past, like Emily Clarkson Moore, George Sisson and Big Jake.

East of Malone and within a stone's throw of the futuristic landscape of giant wind turbines, there's the Cherry Knoll Restaurant, where you can get a great breakfast. For starters, try their French toast with a choice of bacon, sausage or ham and fresh local maple syrup. Red Sox fans beware, however. The dining room décor is chock-a-block New York Yankees memorabilia! You may want to choose your words carefully. And, for a great gathering place, there's the Orchard Side Restaurant, across Route 9 from Chazy Orchards, known far and wide for Champlain Valley McIntosh apples. Every weekday morning, "The Breakfast Club"—about a dozen retirees—congregate for coffee and small talk at Table 7; the regulars serve themselves in their own mugs, which are kept on a shelf just for them. During Lent, for its Friday night fish fries, the restaurant serves perch from Chazy Lake or Lake Champlain to a full house of local patrons. That comes with French fries and cole slaw, with apple crisp or apple pie (made from local Macs of course) for dessert.

The list could go on and on. If you like reliably good food, generous portions and modest prices, try a hometown eatery soon. Besides satisfying your appetite, you can learn a lot about life in the North Country when you eat where the locals eat.

Phil Gallos.

Barry Lobdell.

Phil Gallos.

-Pigeons on barn roofs and metal silo tops-

Lucretia Romey.

Right: *Whit Haynes.*

Below: *WhIt Haynes.*

Lucretia Romey.

A few of the regulars at Lloyd's. *Varick Chittenden.*

Opposite, top: *Debbie Kanze; middle*: *David Pynchon; bottom*: *Tara Freeman.*

Varick Chittenden.

Inside Phillips Diner. *Varick Chittenden.*

A Tom & Jerry at the Crystal. *Varick Chittenden.*

The Bear's Den Trading Post in earlier days. *Courtesy of Tarbell Management Group.*

Martha Cooper.

Jason Hunter/Courtesy of Watertown Daily Times.

Tara Freeman.

Strawberry blossoms. *Jim Bullard.*

Left: *John LaFalce.*

Below: *Amish Farm on Plum Brook Road.* © *Anna Gerhard, from a photograph by Betsy Tisdale.*

Right: *Été*. Diane Leifheit.

Below: Natalia Singer.

Left: Tara Freeman.

Below: Cedar Waxwings.
Brian Henry.

Right: *Lucretia Romey.*

Below: Great Gray
Owl. *Brian Henry.*

Left: Eastern Bluebird. *Brian Henry.*

Below: *Kevin MacKenzie.*

Kevin MacKenzie.

Kevin MacKenzie.

Top: *Tara Freeman*; *middle*: Ice fishing on Lake Champlain. *Betsy Tisdale*; *bottom*: *First Snow. Ken Wiley.*

AT THE RINK

By Paul Graham

For Matt McCluskey and Tom Wilder

A late Friday afternoon in January, the cold snap is here to stay, and I am skating at the outdoor rink with my two friends. For now we have the ice to ourselves. The snowpack amplifies the sunlight, and the breeze kicks up ice crystals that glitter in the air. Behind the rink a softball field sleeps for the winter. Beyond that the Grass River runs fast enough to remain unfrozen at its center.

We skate because we love ice hockey, love the feeling that we have left our bodies behind and for catharsis: from our work, from the confinement of winter itself. Getting out in subfreezing weather is something you must learn to do in the North Country if you are to survive, a difficult lesson to learn because it's counterintuitive, like the advice that you should run *toward* the oncoming CSX freight train if ever your car stalls out on the tracks with the locomotive bearing down. After a few circuits around the rink, though, the blood flows and only my ears feel the bite. Others are sure to arrive soon, men laughing loudly as they pull gear from their truck beds, dress at the benches and then pick up sticks for a game: overgrown boys my age who skate confidently, their strides eating up the ice as they chase the puck.

My friends, who were born in New York and New Hampshire, are much better skaters than I am. I grew up in Maryland, where the winters are balmy and drizzly and nobody skates. I played baseball instead. I had never even put on ice skates until I bought them as a birthday present to myself two years ago. A friendly saleswoman measured me one day after work, her blue eyes shining. She laced me up and told me to stomp my heels to make sure the fit was good and snug. Then I tried the aisles on the blades: three inches taller, I might have been a girl teetering on her first pair of heels. A pair of hockey skates seemed a foolish purchase for a man in his thirties, yet in the rows of sticks and gloves, I smiled like Hans Brinker.

Hans was born poor, and I've come to realize that I was born out of place. In the midst of another long winter, watching my friends glide backward, their legs crossing over smoothly to maintain speed, or watching them build velocity with three powerful quick strides, or lift the pucks with their sticks to tuck them beneath the crossbar with a *thunk!*, I feel certain that I would trade all of the warm Maryland springs I spent on the orange dirt of an infield scooping grounders for a long, cold winter skating on one of the North Country's ponds, in an arena or at an outdoor rink like this one. Ask me in the summer, when I am pitching in the softball league and I'm on my game, the ball zinging from my hand toward the black corner of the plate, and I might answer differently. But my soul is a winter soul, which means that I would take a thousand crystalline days like this one over one humid day in the nineties.

There is still something of the boy left in me, too, which means that I like speed. I skate much faster than I should, crossing my left foot over my right sloppily, at risk of losing control every second. Put a stick in my hands and I am a true liability to myself and everyone else on the ice. I wear a helmet even when I don't have to. One of these days I'm going to get caught with my head down and be knocked out cold.

After we have warmed up a little, we begin passing pucks—first standing on opposite sides of the rink, just getting reacquainted with our sticks and the ice and then trying to hit each other in stride. My blood pumps hopefully; beneath my layers of shirts I begin to sweat. I still cannot shoot very well, but I am, I think, a good passer, confident and accurate, which makes me slightly better than useless as a teammate, perhaps even appealing. I'm not going to hang onto the puck for very long. I'll lose it if I try to get too ambitious, so within seconds of receiving a pass I always look to send it to someone else. I'm unselfish, though by necessity.

When I try to play in the lunchtime pick-up games during the winter months of the school year—"lunchpuck," as it's known on the St. Lawrence University campus where I teach writing and literature—I don't see much action. I desire simply to follow the play, keep up with the skaters and not get hurt. My one friend says I should strive to be a pest, stick-checking anyone who comes near me, but the students are all in their late teens or early twenties, bursting with power and agility. They can even abuse their bodies and still come out to play full-on for an hour, swishing up and down the ice at a breakneck pace. Some of the students are bemusedly pleasant toward me: they slip me the puck and say nothing when I bobble or skate past it and have to loop back because I cannot yet shift my weight around to glide backward effortlessly, the way I do in my dreams. Even when my shot misses the net, their voices remain chipper and encouraging. Once I broke in all alone and attempted to line up a shot for what would have been my first goal on a live goaltender, but somehow the puck rolled off my stick and weakly struck her pads. My teammates, all eighteen-year-olds, would have ridden their own friends ruthlessly, but for me they made allowances, which was almost worse. "It's okay," they said back on the bench, "just unlucky"—and I recognized in their voices the same tone I use in my office when I speak with students about their writing or some literary concept they are struggling with.

To discover a sport as demanding as ice hockey in your thirties is, in a way, an unfortunate thing. Sometimes I think it would have been less frustrating to start playing in my forties or fifties, when my body would be further from the quickness and agility of its youth and unable to remember what a fast learner it used to be. I was never the strongest or best athlete in any game, but I remember being able to perform well enough: I figured out what my role was and filled it, which meant I embraced my limitations. I relied on positioning or deception, as when I pitch, or I relied on study. That was only ten years ago, maybe even less, and while I am far from old my body does not always react the way I still expect it to: I don't get down on ground balls, I tire faster at the pitching rubber, a fall on the ice or a crash into the boards hurts me for real. In short, I have learned to be afraid of my limitations. On the ice, I stop to consider broken bones, torn ligaments, the indisputable message of pain.

It is an axiom, of course, that fear inhibits learning. I see it in the classroom all the time. The ones who play it safe may still grow, but not as much. Knowing this doesn't make it easier for me to take chances.

At the end of this brilliant day in January, though, when others show up at the rink, they are not boys half our age from the campus but men in their thirties, fathers and neighbors who work for the local government or the Department of Public Works or the Corning plant outside of Canton and some alumni of the area colleges who are back home. We come from different places and backgrounds and lives, but here we all speak the same language, even if some of us are more fluent than others. Our work is over; we've been inside all day; it's time for hockey. The sky is turning soft purple, and the sun slides coldly below the horizon, silhouetting the trees, the distant houses with their smoking chimneys, the hills in the nearby park. The temperature already hangs a few degrees below zero, and there is something hauntingly still and beautiful about the evening.

My friends and I end up on different teams, but it doesn't matter. This is a friendly game, the men all good-hearted and generous, happy simply to be touching the puck on free ice outside, which is the best way to play, the cold on our faces and in our fingertips reminding us of hockey's roots on frozen rivers, ponds and flooded backyards. These guys are very good. They skate well, pass with a crisp pop from tape to tape and hit the open spaces in the goal. When someone misses they hoot and holler and razz each other as the play flows in the opposite direction.

Having made the usual apologies for myself to my teammates in advance, I play my game, avoiding the spots where I can get tangled up and fall, trailing the play, circling awkwardly on the back side of the action and waiting for the puck to come my way so I can pass it back to the high slot, where there's a man in a green sweater who could knock a beer can off a fencepost. Then, after fifteen minutes of this, I finally take a shot from close in, watch it flutter past the goaltender's glove and into the back of the net. *Finally*, I think, though the goal is no big deal because it's not pretty and because the others, my friends included, seem to score at will. But I got one, I finally got one. The trance breaks, and suddenly I'm cold, my ankles ache and it's time to go.

I leave my friends behind. When dusk falls, some of the players will shine the lights of their trucks onto the rink and continue playing. They'll far outlast me, quitting in another hour only because they're half frozen and wind-burned and don't want to kill their batteries. I'd like to stay with them, but I know I'd be risking injury and know as well as I drive back to the warm house that there will be many such winters and many such games, that I'm gliding at last into my northern boyhood.

SCATTERED NOTES FROM THE WONDERLANDS OF HOCKEY

By Oscar D. Sarmiento
June, 2013

When my family moved to the North Country from Eugene, Oregon, so I could take a job as a visiting professor at St. Lawrence University, we knew next to nothing about hockey. How could we? Football was the most popular sport in Eugene. Little flags of the Ducks—the football team of the University of Oregon—were everywhere. But we never went to see the team play. My wife, Liliana, and I were spending most of our days changing diapers, taking turns going with Salvador to the playground, reading *The Cat in the Hat*, finishing our PhD courses and then writing our dissertations.

Growing up in Santiago, Chile, I never heard of hockey. The most exotic sport I knew was rugby. It seemed much more foreign than golf, a sport clearly reserved for "the bold and beautiful" Chilean elite. On the other hand, soccer, displaying its mesmerizing mirage of social mobility for the poor, was as popular as an American peanut butter sandwich.

But I didn't play much soccer as a youth, and I wasn't a fanatical follower of the sport. One thing that was fun about street soccer was the ingenious ways kids had for making soccer balls. With a bit of imagination, anything—a newspaper, a can of soda, a plastic bottle—could be made into a soccer ball. I blamed my lack of passion for the sport on flat feet. My lack of skill could really hurt my fragile youthful ego. One time, a cousin invited me to play a friendly game with kids three years my juniors. At first my height and savvy demeanor made a strong impression on them, but upon seeing me running like a desperado behind the ball, they realized that I couldn't dribble.

Fast-forward a few decades, and lo and behold, Salvador, son of a non-dribbler, is playing baseball, soccer and hockey, and also snowboarding!

When our family came to the North Country, Sal was four years old. In Oregon, playgrounds had been plentiful and the weather mild if rainy, a comparative paradise. Sal had spent endless hours playing outside; rain never stopped him from getting on his tricycle and pedaling to the closest playground or house to meet up with friends. One telling picture of those days shows Salvador smiling, his eyes sparkling full of wicked life, posing next to his imposing tricycle—a perfect three-year-old James Dean.

But, we quickly learned, playgrounds were not a year-round proposition in the North Country. So it was not long before Sal was ice skating at Appleton Arena in Canton.

The decision to sign him up for some skating lessons was a no-brainer. He would engage with other kids, release some of his ebullient energy and learn new skills. And there we were, inside the ice arena in Canton, with other parents, in the thick of winter, watching our kids standing up like ducks on their skating boots and slowly learning to slide on their own on the ice.

Years later, after Salvador had played hockey for a long time, one of his coaches asked me almost casually when my son had started skating. I realized how important it had been for Salvador to start early, because most dedicated kids on hockey teams are put on skates as soon as they can stand up. That first winter at Appleton Arena, however, when I saw him go around the rink with other children, it didn't dawn on me that we had brought Salvador to the core of the North Country—the frozen radiance of a rink where boot blades meet the ice and the heart of a boy glimmers to the beat of a winter sun.

What also took place that winter, while Sal started to skate, was our getting acquainted, if briefly, with other parents. The hours spent at the rink gave Liliana and me a chance to chat the snow away, drink hot chocolate and try something new, some—yikes!—French fries with vinegar. The warmth of conversations and simple laughs tempered the sense of isolation we felt under a snowy and chilly winter. It was at Appleton Arena that we met Bruce and Noli (short for Magnolia), who had also brought their son, Kenny, to the rink. Bruce was an engineer working for a paper mill two hours by car from Canton. The two had met when he, after college, had spent a year in Guatemala as a Peace Corps volunteer. For us, finding someone from Guatemala in that Canton rink was more surprising than finding a needle in a haystack.

I told a college colleague about these friends we were visiting and seeing constantly. "Who are they?" he asked me. "Do your friends work for the college?"

"No," I told him. "They are from town." The puzzled look on his face made it clear to me that this friendship was rare and unique, that it was a gift.

It did not take long for Salvador to get used to skating around the rink. We knew this would happen, because when it came to making new friends and playing, he was all action and no trepidation. Taking him to the arena was fun for the whole family.

Other parents saw ice skating as just the beginning of a tenacious journey. Many were already planning to encourage their kids to play hockey for years to come. But the turn our lives would take after that first year of ice skating did not dawn on me right away. I guess my student life in Eugene, Oregon, where going to the Saturday market to watch colorful hippie life blossoming was a major thrill, had not prepared me well for a hockey journey. Salvador, on the other hand, had found a great way to enjoy the ice and make new friends.

Watching him so enthusiastically pick up hockey was almost surreal. Little kids skating in padded helmets reminded me of astronauts floating in outer space. My son's prior sheer delight in sliding loosely around the rink had to turn now into a more efficient and team-oriented effort.

Pressed in the back of my mind was the certainty that sports were part of leisure, something I could deeply enjoy because my participation was casual. But an organized community sport was not, as I was to learn, necessarily casual; quite to the contrary, it was arranged in such a way as to force all activities to fit into a plan of long-term family commitment. For Sal, going to hockey practice was not a burden, but one more exhilarating occasion to meet with friends—all those shining blue, black and green helmets switching places like hornets along the rink—and channel his energy. Now he not only needed his helmet and skates (whose blades I had to remind myself to get sharpened from time to time); he also needed gear that would protect him from the potential injuries that come with any contact sport. No matter what, he would put on his helmet, his shin guards, his elbow pads and his shoulder pads. Smiling, he would wait patiently for me to lace up his skates. The most annoying part of the whole routine was fastening his long hockey socks by taping them to each leg. We were happy if we had not left anything at home, which happened from time to time. Standing tall on his skates, hockey stick in hand, Salvador would burst out of the locker room ready to show off his high spirits and start his practice drills.

My son's coaches would instruct him on how to gain speed on the ice, carry the puck and pass it fast to a teammate. The puck, as I would discover, could fly from one corner to the other like a lightning bolt. His coaches were all men who as children and teenagers had played with passion. Some of them had even played in college. Most were coaching at least one of their children. Life was going full circle for them. Not for me, certainly, because I had always been more into reading books, learning languages or playing my guitar. Perhaps my son would have enjoyed more having a father ready to go out and play with him than one who painstakingly read Ezra Pound or French philosopher Jacques Derrida for hours.

Each practice would start with a number of drills. Kids would speed from one side of the rink to the other. They would skate the length of the rink, passing the puck to each other, and shoot the puck to the goalie. Before some playing time at the end, they had to start making a disciplined effort to train themselves to become more technically crafty. In turn, parents had to become more concerted cheerleaders of their children's efforts.

As we were to learn, parents were the driving force behind hockey teams. Coaches were like robust orchestra conductors, showing their charges both how to turn into alert ice skaters and also how to apply full concentrated effort to perform as an organized team, but parents' support was at the heart of the kids' vitality and love for the sport. Securing all the gear and having them ready to get to the rink on time was just the start. Among other things, parents also had to take turns at the arena snack bar selling food and coffee, participate in fundraising raffles, drive early in the morning or at night to out-of-town arenas and generally devote many hours only to hockey. Some of these parents were single mothers or fathers. Some had recently divorced. How did they manage to juggle work and hockey every week?

During the years in which Salvador played, my wife and I were untenured assistant professors at SUNY Potsdam, teaching four courses per semester, participating in Faculty Senate committees, presenting at conferences, writing articles for publication in academic journals and much more. Extraordinarily, rather than driving the three of us insane from October to March, the hockey season kept my family engaged and focused. Granted, it may have been exhausting, but it was never dull.

Parents enjoyed being at the arena. Giving of their time to hockey was worthwhile because they wanted to provide their kids with the mental and physical discipline that participating in sports offers. Some of them—the most ambitious—probably dreamed of seeing their kids going off to college to play, or perhaps make it to a professional league, even the NHL. They all wanted to keep their kids physically active, entertained and mentally alert. We all relished the chance to share life experiences with folks other than our coworkers. Where else could my wife and I have met parents who volunteered for rescue squads and parents who were placing buoys in the St. Lawrence River? One father told us he had once dragged a corpse from one of the rivers in the region. A vehicle had gone through the ice, and the driver had drowned.

We also met some grandparents at the arena; this was especially rewarding for us, being so far away from our own parents and relatives. If being around children and people our age was fun, being around elderly people was emotionally nurturing. Talking to them was like talking respectfully, but also as friends, to our own grandparents. The arena, in short, allowed us to have a glimpse of true family life in the North Country.

As parents, we made sure to let our kids know that we were fully rooting for them. My son's team would play games all over the North Country and beyond. One of these locations was, on occasion, Akwesasne, the Mohawk reservation on the St. Lawrence River. Where had they been all this time, all those Native American boys racing all over the rink? Their solid shapes reflected back onto my own existence, a brown Hispanic man "lost" in a sea of townsfolk. Finding that there was a place in the North Country where Mohawk kids could shine forth was an exhilarating, moving surprise. While rooting for my son's team, I also found myself silently rooting for the Akwesasne boys we were playing against, because I did not want those boys to lose.

We would play at several arenas in Canada. After living for a while in the North Country, I discovered that, though people live very close to Canada, not many cross the border and so do not get acquainted with two wonderful cities I was eager to visit, Ottawa and Montreal. I wonder now how many of the hockey parents got to know only the arenas where we played games and never spent a weekend getting to know those cities. To my delight, it was easy for the border officers to tell that our reason for going to Canada was a hockey game—my son was almost fully dressed in his hockey gear, and the equipment bag and sticks were prominent features in the back of our car. Though I had an accent and could not pass for your regular North Country man—these were the good times, before 9/11—"hockey" worked like a charm, opening both gates standing in front of me: the gate to enter Canada and the one to return to the United States.

As they grew, our children progressed from playing different team positions to one that was to be theirs for the rest of the season. This process was as trying for my wife and me as it was for other parents. Sal was becoming an excellent player, and we thought he deserved to play forward, giving him chances to score, stand out and obtain the personal and public recognition we thought he certainly deserved. From time to time, Sal did play forward, but most often he was a defender. Like all parents, we wanted our son to be appreciated and celebrated for how well he was playing, regardless of his role; congratulating him genuinely was not very difficult because, given the chance, he would prove that he was an outstanding player by moving fast around the rink, carrying the puck through a maze of players and passing it to those who could have a chance to score or keep moving the puck forward.

But perhaps what was most salient about his playing was that he was a very considerate player who played the game for the sake of doing well and having fun and not to hurt players from opposing teams. He could tell the difference between playing effectively according to the rules and getting obnoxious and hurting other players. As a defender it was his duty to check some players against the boards when it was necessary; this could result in some kid needing a respite to be able to breathe naturally again. But I don't recall any instance in which Sal checked simply to vent his anger.

For a brief period, Sal worried us because he insisted on becoming his team's goalie. Awful news. The goalie, probably the most demanding position in hockey, and such a daunting responsibility! Liliana and I knew very well that the brunt of a defeat falls like a ton of bricks on the goalie's shoulders. Also, the goalie, though he trains along with all the players and learns to sharpen his skills as much as any other player, stays in the same place for the entire time he is on the ice. The goalie stays put (or so I pictured him in my fretful mind), like a snowman—Godot?—waiting for somebody who shall never arrive to save him from…himself!

So there were plenty of reasons for us not to want Sal playing goalie. Most of all, we wanted him skating as much as possible, exerting himself physically and enjoying the thrill of being part of a very fast-paced sport. Goalie? That was a four-letter word.

At the time, as savvy parents, we didn't argue too much, but we didn't encourage Sal to become a goalie either. We already knew that saying no to our son would immediately raise plenty of red flags, so, we thought, to keep our cool was the best move. Was not that also part of being a good middle-class American family, keeping one's cool? Other kids also wanted to be goalie, and, to our huge relief, they and not Sal ended up playing in that position.

This said, I do recall how painful it was for a while for a friend, a single mother, to be the parent of the team's goalie. Her boy was perhaps not the fastest on the ice, and not unlike Sal, he probably thought that a perfect way to stand out from the crowd was to become the goalie. At least that was my reading of the situation. (Do we as adults do the same at times, I wonder, and make sorrowful fools of ourselves? I am afraid we do it more often than we dare to recognize. But when a child does it, it can be endearing.) Our friend was stressing out each time her son, our brand-new goalie, was on the ice. And though he did gain the respect of his teammates through willpower and a cheerful spirit—because he was a real gutsy little fellow—I saw that the painful realization of our team's defeats hit him harder than it did most kids.

In the end, as hockey seasons came and went, Sal ended up playing in one of the two defense positions. The coaches made their decision and trained him hard and smart, so Sal was playing alongside crafty defenders. Could we have convinced them otherwise? Could a father who had never played hockey or even ice skated have any say in the matter? Unlikely. I should have known from the first day that Sal stepped on the ice that were he to stay with hockey as a teenager, he would have to be disciplined, and that, not less than his coaches, I would have to instill that discipline, as I had it instilled in me when, still in my teen years, I studied classical guitar and learned that you have to make choices and accept that some activities that others enjoy will not be there for you.

Sal developed a keen sense of teamwork and cooperation. He refined his skills. The more he grew as a hockey player, the more we understood how the responsibility to play well, to be mentally and physically ready on the ice and to be part of a well-oiled machine weighed on him and his teammates. More and more, the outcome of a game depended on each individual's contribution to the energy fueling the team.

Perhaps one of the more enduring lessons from my son's involvement in hockey was that focused passion is at the core of the game. That passion can turn into something dangerous when the rules are not respected, and kids suffer the consequences. I do not recall Sal ever getting injured on the ice as a result of an opponent's foul move. Passion, however, can become aggression, both on the rink and next to it, among the parents. What kept us vigilant about remaining gracious was the fact that our team was made up of kids who were learning the ropes of the game and had parents who, regardless of where they lived or how they fit into society, were all eager to secure opportunities for growth for their kids.

I still see Sal skating back at the speed of light to defend his goal. It was especially hard seeing him defending when his team was losing, because a lot of physical and psychological pressure was put on defense players when this was happening. On occasion our kids instantly lost heart when they saw the other team scoring on them. From the outside, as parents, this reaction was achingly obvious to us. We knew that unless their team spirit regained some vitality they would be unable to return full throttle to the game to courageously win it. In circumstances such as these it was evident that our kids were just that, kids playing a game, kids growing up, kids with hearts and hopes and not warrior-machines eager to crush some opponents. Our children needed solid, explicit encouragement from us.

And so the cheerleading made more and more sense to me. At times, though, I wondered if we were pushing our kids into a chauvinistic mold that would turn them into silly warriors. Sports—and hockey is one telling example—can be much more than that, because they teach us lessons of discipline, joy, fraternity and exhilaration, especially when in a game that seemed lost for good our kids would prove that they could, under very trying circumstances and out of sheer determination and skill, make a quick comeback and win. Magic was the name of hockey right then and there.

Of the many unique kids who played along with Sal over the years, two come to mind for different reasons: Elizabeth and Matt. Elizabeth was the only girl on my son's team for years, until, when they all became teenagers, she started playing with an all-female team. She had deep black eyes, long black hair and lots of freckles. And was she able to stand her ground! At first, she seemed to be a cute addition to the team. When the kids were older, she became a strong and dynamic spirit thriving on being her own on the rink, fighting for her team and clearly supported by her teammates. I do not remember her backing down under pressure; she was fast and driven, a tough and smart player. At times, I had the impression that Elizabeth's strong presence on the ice frustrated her peers' attempts at forming a full-of-bravado boys' crowd.

Her dad and I had plenty of occasions to talk about simple things. He brought Elizabeth to practice, at times helped coach the team, encouraged his daughter to do her best and smiled, smiled, smiled.

Matt stood out because he, who grew up to be an excellent player, kept his cool at heated times when I would not have done so at his age. On those occasions his blood must have been boiling beneath his calm demeanor. Not that Matt was the only kid sitting quietly for what seemed hours collapsed into minutes, waiting for his shift; this was a lesson that all players had to learn and relearn. But for me, he became the telling example of a boy who really loves the sport and will go against the impetus of his rushing blood to stay focused and wait, wait, wait. Discipline in action: that's what Matt embodied for me.

Most kids, Sal included, stopped playing hockey either before or during high school and went on to other things, to study in college, to help their parents, to experience life. Matt was bent on playing hockey; later he played in college with other kids from town. Many must have envied him. Matt, who was always a cute boy, blossomed into a handsome teenager, dated some of the prettiest girls in high school and attained the status of a semi-celebrity. Yet he never acted snotty about his talent, his looks or his dates. I believe that his dad helped Matt keep things in perspective. Like other loving fathers, Matt's would come dutifully to see his son play and, no matter what, find—or so it seemed to me—a way to arrange his work shifts to make it to the practices and games. He—and also his wife surely—realized how much depended on his active involvement with his son's playing. He knew that the stakes were becoming higher as the kids were turning into thriving teenagers. Positive that his son had real talent for the sport, Matt's dad would steer him gently and firmly toward learning more and practicing more and would teach him the value of patience.

A laugh or a brief hilarious remark indicated to my wife and me how much Matt's dad had to collect himself at times to cultivate his son's spirit. Being a hockey dad meant fully embodying the fatherly role so as to teach something of value to our boys through their behavior in the rink. My wife and I understood this quickly. Salvador had to trust that his patience would pay off and wait for his turn to play. For us, taking residence in the North Country meant to keep our eyes open, our hearts receptive and truly go with the flow, adjusting to and enjoying the circumstances. Matt's dad was probably the model hockey father: courteous, constantly volunteering but without going overboard, friendly to everybody, a nice person to talk to and clearly unpretentious. I was starting to work on my smile.

One episode when our involvement in hockey proved crucial to the well-being of my family was the devastating ice storm of January 1998. With no electricity, along with many other families in similar conditions, we spent two excruciating days in Maxcy Hall, SUNY Potsdam's athletics facility.

We could have stayed longer had we not been fortunate enough to get an invitation from a couple whose son was playing hockey with Salvador. When they found out that we were out of our house and at the gymnasium, they immediately invited us to brave the rest of the ordeal with them at their house. They had electricity!

This couple not only welcomed us, but they also made sure to let my wife and me sleep in their bed and provided us with warm food and casual, pleasant conversation. There was no reason for them to do so other than kindness and friendship nurtured at our sons' hockey games. We made sure to send them a bouquet of flowers once we were back in our house and life had returned to normal.

When Salvador stopped playing hockey, he was already at the midget level. He decided that the time had come to do other things. We could have insisted he continue for one more year, but we did not. His coach was looking forward to having him on the team and approached him, but Sal was tired and upset after a long season on three different teams. Unlike some fathers, I never saw hockey as a way for my son to become a professional or even semi-professional athlete. I saw his participation as an activity that was fun, educational and healthy. As he continued I saw that the game was becoming more and more competitive and that more than playing simply for the sake of playing was at stake. My view was, perhaps, shortsighted.

On the other hand, a boy whose father had never seen hockey throughout his life was, of all things conceivable on this planet, turning into a fast, smart hockey player. I had abundant evidence when we went to play in a state hockey tournament. More than playing, both teams were dancing furiously on the ice. There was, it seemed, no respite, no place for a mistake, only time flowing in full, and the kids, all of them, spending every trace of energy left in their bodies on the game. I had never seen my son play so deftly, displaying such intelligence and skill, skating like a speeding bullet.

The stakes were high for Sal's team; they could go to the next round and play against a team from another state. But, more personally, that day the stakes, I thought, were particularly high for my son. He had to pull together all he had learned throughout the years and play at his best not only against superb opposition but also alongside a teammate who was good enough to go on to play professionally.

Salvador did not flinch. He was all concentration, technique, passion and speed. For me, the many years he had played the sport, the many coaches who had trained him and the many parents cheering for the team time and again were right there inspiring him to go beyond what he thought he could possibly give of himself to the sport. Considering his dad's absolute lack of acquaintance with the sport prior to coming to the North Country and the complete devotion of other fathers to the sport, my son's play that day was truly amazing.

I had come to this country, and then the North Country, intending to share my love for the guitar and perhaps poetry with Salvador. Through hockey I have come to understand and appreciate the passion others have for sports. I could not have found myself in a more unpredictable situation in my immigrant life with a son who was gifted in so many areas.

Looking back, I remember as endearing those times when our kids were not yet teenagers. The beauty of their glimmering eyes and faces mesmerized by the puck and the stick in their small hands reminds me that I was also once a little boy looking forward to meeting with my friends after school just to joke, to get worked up about trivialities, always ready to play and play and play. Playing gave us, as it did my son, the living certainty that one belonged in a small, thriving, noisy, inspiring community of peers. Though I might have suspected at times that my son was being trained to fit into a prototypical aggressive masculine mold, I also sensed that he had enough freedom to let loose, to be himself, to mess up, to try and try and try. And try his best at hockey Salvador did.

INVISIBLE PEOPLE

By Jill Vaughan

They're gone, the whole bunch of them. I'd always known they weren't visible to everyone, but I never expected them to recede from my view the way they have.

For almost twenty years I'd worked with the poorest people in Franklin County: the people on Public Assistance. I'd known the dynamics of their families and known their children's dispositions and teachers. I'd talked to them and written letters to them. I'd championed them, been angry with them and had my heart broken by the hopelessness of their situations.

And now, they're gone.

I switched jobs. I thought I'd see them around. But I don't. They are the invisible people. They have no transportation, and it's winter. Someone's posture on a sidewalk will call my attention, and I'll realize it is someone who was on my caseload. Now and again I'll see a jacket that's familiar. But the jackets will eventually be thrown out or outgrown, and people will be anonymous bodies with heads bent into the cold.

I knew they were dispossessed. I knew they didn't shop or attend school concerts. But wouldn't our paths intersect somewhere? No. They don't have warm clothes, and their personal ecology is not to seek out the cold and uncomfortable; they're facing enough inner stress. Garage-sale strollers don't work in the snow, and who has money for winter clothes for the kids?

I thought they might call me, was worried I'd be overwhelmed. I forgot how inured they are to loss and abandonment. There's no sense wasting energy on anything but mute acceptance. Feelings are something to put a lid on, if possible. Grief is self-indulgent, and loneliness is dangerous.

I still know where they live—the kitchens I've sat in hundreds of times and the crowded porches where extra people sleep or stuff is piled. But maybe they don't live there anymore. They have no permanent addresses. Phone numbers and houses shift like fog.

They're gone—no, I'm gone. I removed myself from their universe; they're still there. I am close enough that I still see some faces, still hear some conversations, but the connections are loosening—the time is late and the sounds are fading. I feel the goodbye in my mind and feel the absence in my soul.

This commentary made its first public appearance on North Country Public Radio on January 23, 2009.

Part III

The Flora and the Fauna

Thanks for reading!.
Nancy

GARDEN LEGACY: THE REAL DIRT

By Nancy Berbrick

In the North Country, the season for gardening is short. My grandmother always told me that it never did much good to put your garden in until after Memorial Day. It's tempting, though; in a matter of a couple of early warm days, the hills go from the dead grays and tin-type sepia tones of winter to every hue of green—lush. The leaf buds burst, and it's spring—at least it looks like spring. We're not fooled. It will be almost two months yet before anything tender can go out.

But, being the hardy souls of the North, we find ways: black plastic bags around the outsides of the tomato cages with balls of newspaper over the tops when (not if) it turns really cold again. Sensitive melons can sometimes survive early cold snaps under little paper garden caps. I've planted potatoes in old tires, covered them with dirt, then stacked another tire on top, filled that one, and again, to get the earliest potatoes ever. I've started things in cold frames with milk bottles full of water and painted black to catch the occasional early spring sunshine and warmth. I've built cold frames of hay bales and old windows and covered short rows with recycled plastic tunnels.

In the fall it's the same. We cover crops with old sheets, shower curtains, blankets, newspapers, whatever we have. Night after frosty night we baby our gardens so that we can have a few more weeks, a few more days, of beautiful flowers and fresh delicious vegetables, or until we can find enough time to take care of whatever abundance is left.

My love for gardening is probably buried somewhere in my genetic code. My grandmother could grow just about anything. I still have patches of rhubarb and red sedum, fancy hens and chickens and bleeding heart that she gave me years before she died. Every spring my mother starts dozens of pieces of an old variegated impatiens plant we've had going for years. She gives each of her six children rooted and potted slips. Our plants have been passed down from generation to generation, a sort of poor family legacy, I guess. That ivy came from great-grandma's wedding bouquet or this flourishing raspberry patch came from grandma, who would say, "Nan, my raspberries are escaping! If you want some, come and dig them."

When I was young, my mother decided she wanted some blueberries. She took an old sheet and herded my brothers and sisters and me down the hill to the park where we gathered the red, gold, yellow and orange colors of fall, mountains of maple and oak leaves, and dragged the bulging sheet back up the hill to use as mulch and to condition the soil. For the same purpose, from the forest across the road, we filled our little red wagon with prickly rust-colored pine needles, our hands blackening from the pitch. When the soil was acidic enough, she dug a few wild plants and transplanted them carefully. After all these years, our lips still turn purple as we feast.

Another time, my mother cleared a shady bank behind a decaying outbuilding in the backyard, pulling thistles, poison ivy and nettles to make a flower bed. She couldn't afford to buy plants so she collected them—ferns, Dutchman's britches, jack-in-a-pulpits, trilliums (or, as we called them, stink pots)—all protected plants now and maybe even then. But she dug them, carried them home and lovingly tended them, and they thrived.

Eventually, my mother gave each one of us a garden of our own to tend. Mine ran down along a stone wall. Sweet peas twined among the rocks, and a mock orange bush flowered on the corner. There a tiny yellow bird built a nest at eye-level, while small garter snakes slithered among the stones in the fence. The only time the snakes bothered me was when I accidentally stepped on one in my bare feet—startling both of us. I loved that garden and spent hours pulling weeds and scratching around the plants. Pretty much everything in a family our size was shared, but this place was mine.

Most kids, when they go off to college, leave the whole gardening thing behind. I, on the other hand, became the gardener in the huge apartment complex in Rochester, New York, where I lived while attending classes. It was a way to help pay the rent, a way to keep my hands in the soil. So I planted and tended about fifty flower boxes in the spring and dug weeds out of a central flower bed in the summer. I managed to find a piece of dirt to plant some vegetables on, and when I started to harvest, I had more than I could possibly use. My city neighbors were amazed when they found bags of fresh vegetables outside their doors. I invited all the families in our building to a watermelon party, and we became good friends.

At times gardening has gotten me into a little trouble. From the apartment complex, I moved into a mobile home community where we all had very nice homes on house-sized lots—plenty of room for a garden! The problem was that when the community was built the top-soil was all bulldozed away, leaving only hardpan clay. Somehow, I found a friend of a friend who piled a whole dump-truck load of composted cow manure on my newly paved driveway. It took two weeks to wheelbarrow it all to the back of the yard.

The neighbors were not happy.

Something else that they didn't like was when I collected bags of grass clippings on garbage day. They made great compost, but I have to admit, they did reek for a few days. Still, by the time I moved back home to the North Country I had the most beautiful and productive garden in the whole neighborhood. Ironically, a friend called me shortly after I moved to tell me that everyone was taking boxes and wheelbarrow loads of soil from my abandoned garden.

A few years later, I found myself raising four children on a small dairy farm in St. Lawrence County. The equipment was old and broken down, the herd was made up of cull cows and there was no money. I had never lived on a farm, but I knew how to cultivate plants. My garden grew from a little scrap to about a quarter of an acre. In the summer we had lettuce, cucumbers, peppers, onions, garlic and herbs. Strawberries, melons, raspberries and grapes satisfied our fruit cravings. If we had nothing else, we had food— hundreds of quarts of tomatoes, beans, carrots, corn, beets, grape juice and jams, along with all sorts of pickles and relishes.

I didn't forget the flowers, either. Hollyhocks hid the cracks in the foundation of our house. Inherited perennials—peonies, lilacs, painted daisies—snuggled into sunny spaces. Hostas—silver, buttercup, earth angels—graced the shade. The ditches overflowed with lilies—lemon and tiger. I seeded in pansies, pinks and asters. My days were filled with dirty, backbreaking work, but when I had a few minutes I would take my youngest daughter, a toddler, and sit among my flowers, breathing the sweet herbal scents, feeling the warmth of the sun, hearing the buzzing of the bees busy at their gathering. I would scratch around and pull a few weeds, and Sarah would dig with a little spoon. That was my place of comfort and peace where I could escape for a few moments from the grueling farm chores.

My kids took it for granted that practically everything came from the garden. In the evening after we had finished our chores, I would take a stroll around the garden, often accompanied by one or more of my children. My three-year-old twin son Adam and I were admiring the garden one evening. Suddenly he looked up at me, startled, and asked, "Mom, where do people in the city get their food?"

"Where do you think they get their food?"

He thought for a few seconds. His eyes widened, and he said, "They must have to go to the store!" A few days later Aaron, his twin, came running up to tell me that his brother was chewing *gum* that he had found in the garden. I had to explain that even *we* get *gum* from the store!

I can't say that my children had any great love for the hard work of that quarter-acre. They dutifully cleared their assigned rows, where sometimes the weeds grew taller than they were. Certain favorites received extra care, while none of them wanted to put any of their efforts into the asparagus. "We hope that dies, Mom!" they said. I never *could* get them to eat more than the required teaspoon-sized no-thank-you helping of that vegetable.

After we moved into town, the garden shrank down to fit the small backyard. As teenagers, my kids didn't pay much attention to it, and I thought the garden legacy was finished. But after college, when Adam moved to a western city he called to tell me that his neighbors were all impressed at the huge tomato crop he'd grown in a bucket outside his apartment door. He told me he *bottled* six quarts! (We'd say *canned*.) At my daughter's home, I discovered a weedy little patch where a couple of tomatoes, a few bean plants and even a cucumber vine struggled. In the process of tidying it up a bit, I found that Kendra's two-year-old son loves to dig, pull weeds and, especially, eat raw green beans and broccoli.

These days, even I get distracted and sometimes wonder why I bother with all the work that the garden entails. But after my youngest daughter was married and she and her husband bought the house next door, we decided to share a garden. We're both busy in our lives and don't get to work in it together very often. I'll come home, and she will have weeded a couple of rows. Sometimes I'll harvest and leave half at her door, or she'll harvest and leave half at mine. She loves digging around in her flowers, and she loves the healthy fresh vegetables and fruits.

She inherited my grandmother's name, and last year I gave her some of that variegated impatiens. She planted it next to that little patch of grandma's rhubarb.

HEART BERRY

By Heather Horning

Walking among strawberry fields with my grandmother, the sugary scent of the air lightens me. I need to feel love again.

My wise grandmother grasps my hand, and the last few chosen berries fall into the woven basket at my elbow. Holding her gaze for a final moment, I feel the last few months of winter pass through me, to her and away. Spring has finally returned. The strawberries tell me. This sweet berry whispers a message in my ear, telling me that with new life comes new love, and I will be born anew. I have only to trust the fruits, the gifts of my Creator and let go.

As I walk across that gentle green meadow, to share with my grandmother a simple moment together, I'm not thinking about the gifts all around me. I am focused inward. The harsh months of winter in the North Country have taken their toll, and I have pulled away from everything, from everyone who cares about me.

Meeting with my mother's mother once more in the fields for a fresh bonding experience, I feel a strange tingling sensation enter my body. The fruits of my childhood, the same ones that had dampened my youthful tongue as my grandma gazed down at me from under her clear bonnet, call my name—Heather, from the soil of my own culture, part of me that I'd forgotten reaches out for the promise of a new spring. I need this new beginning, more than I've ever needed anything in my life. Taking my grandmother's hands in my own, the tears fall one by one to the earth beneath my toes, and I feel the heart berry begin to grow within me once more—painful, bittersweet, but a natural part of rebirth and the cycle of life.

—◦◦◦—

There is a ceremony that truly honors this gift of nature, the strawberry. It helps the people rejoice in the unadulterated gifts of Mother Nature. It honors the people who pick the strawberries and give back to the earth in the continuation of their families through the female line. It is part and parcel of the *Haudenosaunee*, known to many as the Iroquois peoples.

James Herrick writes that the strawberry "possess[es] great amounts of power" because of its wild, natural qualities. According to Katsi Cook, this "leader of the berries" exemplifies how the fruit itself deserves to be revered. It is a significant part of several Iroquois recipes. When it arrives as the first nourishing food of the new spring season, this bright flash of red life serves as an awakening to the people long dormant in winter. I consider this as I take the steps into my childhood grassland, just off the path to my grandmother's home.

Conversely, an individual who has had a recent brush with death might claim that he or she "almost ate strawberries." I almost ate strawberries. Looking back now, I thank my own God that I am tasting real, live berries instead. I think this comes partly from the belief that, hopefully, the world of the Iroquois peoples' Creator will be laden with strawberries. The strawberry on Earth is generally known to have strong medicinal qualities. Strawberries are not only succulent and scrumptious but also help in "maintaining and restoring the general welfare of individuals or groups of individuals," writes Herrick. It is also a natural, wild being, coming from nature as people do; allowing both to work together creates harmony.

I have found, finally, in this rebirth, a fledgling strength. When I work with the strawberries, I find a passion that has long been dormant. I revisit that passion, as the moisture fades from my vision and my knees sink into the cool earth once more. I think.

After the winter, when the Strawberry Ceremony is held, the fruit is the perfect solution to the slumber of the long, hard months of cold weather. The strawberry gives new life to the people after the winter's sleep. The ripe red berry is rich with iron, which can help with anemia induced by winter. Iron, along with magnesium, potassium and sodium in the berry, leaves and roots, acts as a blood purifier and builder. All parts of the wild fruit are useful, some as laxative, diuretic or astringent.

These cleansing properties can also be used in accordance with women's needs. During "moon time," pregnancy or following childbirth, the strawberry can be eaten to cleanse the woman's body, which is generally believed to be highly toxic during these times.

I keep these aspects in mind as I gently ease into the mechanics of picking—and eating. The strawberries are cleansing my body, I think. I believe. This is why they are the first natural fruit of the eastern spring. It is meant to be. And I have waited a long while for this moment to arrive. I feel the assurance of the fruit caressing my fingers…

After the long winter, the *Haudenosaunee* celebration of the strawberry calls the people into nature again, much like the sunshine and clear breaths of air pull my grandmother and me back into my life. Women and children, sometimes accompanied by men, go on picnicking parties all throughout the month of June, collecting the wild strawberries in their woven splint baskets to bring home to make into syrup, bread, drink and anything else imaginable.

These "berry-picking excursions provided occasion for much merry gossip" as well, Cook points out. During the ceremony, people socialize as they pick the berries. All celebrate the nourishing present of the new year. Along with this merriment, though, they confess their sins and commence forgiveness of their fellow creatures. Whatever unhappiness has taken place over the preceding months is now allowed into the open and all are cleansed mentally, emotionally and spiritually as the physical body is decontaminated.

Rediscovery. I love that moment between my grandmother and myself each new spring. This time, though, I have more difficulty sharing. The strawberries enliven my spirit in short and tender bursts.

Talk about a lesson I need to learn. As I breathe in the tart scent and feel the liquid aroma stroke my tongue, I feel my body begin to relax, to let go of some of the pain. I revisit the past, from childhood dreams to womanly desires—love in the form of nature and of fruit. The renewal of the heart berry, both within and around me, brings floods of memories to my eyes, memories that I want to exalt in and yet suppress as I touch my spirit in that strawberry field, all the while knowing that my grandmother watches over, keeping me safe. I desperately require this time to heal, and she knows it. The world around me knows it.

—◦◦◦—

As I share my story, I find my spirit creating parallels once more to the *Haudenosaunee* culture. A storyteller opens his lips and tells a story of his people, a tale that speaks of a time when the strawberry, heart-shaped, heals the emotionally wounded heart.

A husband offended his wife, who put his things outside their lodge door, effectively divorcing him. The man, "wounded to the core" because of his mistake, realized that he really did love his wife and needed to regain her trust. He went to the Creator and asked what he should do. The Creator gave the man seeds and told him to plant them along the path the woman trod to the river to get water.

The man did as he was told and waited for the plant to grow. But when it did, it was scraggly, with no fruit. The wife saw this plant and claimed that it "looks like something nasty my husband did." Her husband was not invited back into the longhouse; he was "demolished."

The man returned to the Creator and thanked him but also said that the seed had not worked. The Creator told the man that he had planted the seeds incorrectly and gave him more seeds to try.

The man did as he was told, planting the new seeds next to the scraggly bush. These took root and grew vigorously. By the time the wife went to get more water, their white blossoms had turned into ruby-red strawberries. When the woman passed, she exclaimed, "Look at all the hearts on these plants! It must have been a very good person who planted these. What a pity it wasn't my husband who planted these to show me his love." At this, the husband leaped out from behind the bush to tell his wife that he had indeed planted them for her. The wife welcomed her husband back, with open arms and a happy heart.

The strawberry in the Eastern spring brings new life, a new heart to the people of the earth. The Creator, giver of the gift of strawberries, knows their power to restore love and so caused them to be shaped like the human heart. The story shows that women recognize the power of the strawberry; the wife sees all the "hearts" on the plants as symbols of the living, beating regulator of life. The reunion heals both spouses' hearts by giving them new ones in the embodiment of the fruit. Spring, thanks to the Creator, always brings new life, forgiveness, cleansing and new love—all wrapped up together in a simple reminder of fertility.

—◦◦◦—

As my basket fills, I look up again, to witness the sunset on this beautiful day. Thinking so deeply about my life, remembering those stories in the midst of this nurturing spring, I experience peace. Glancing up, I see my grandmother straighten, her basket full as well. Her smile glistens in the last rays of the light. She knows the power of the strawberry. That's why she brought me here.

Wild strawberries hibernate for the winter—and some don't come back strong in spring. And so with our hearts. Mine couldn't make it until I could meet my grandmother on the open field once more and be enclosed in her esteemed embrace. She and my mother expect little from me but to be their granddaughter and daughter. For now, as I stand in the mist of fresh air and the passion of the sun, I am enough. Even though I am only beginning to regrow, I recognize that I am part of something larger than myself. I am a small but significant part of this creation. I am part of a cycle. I am my grandmother's child, and someday I will have a daughter of my own. Though that future isn't so clear now, I know that I can trust the tradition of my family to see me through. Someday I'll be picking the strawberries with my own child, maybe even with a granddaughter. But we'll be doing more than picking berries. We'll be laughing, grieving, hugging and loving. And I'm finally realizing, as the warm spring sun lights my face, that though I'm afraid to love again, terrified to give my heart again, it will happen. It's a part of this big cycle to which we belong.

DOG DAYS IN THE NORTH COUNTRY

By Natalia Rachel Singer

It's the first day of August, a golden Saturday after a gray summer of rain, when my husband and I set out for Blue Mountain Lake with our dog, Zoë, an Australian shepherd mix. When we adopted her six years ago from the Potsdam Humane Society, she was eight weeks old. Back then she had blue eyes and weighed eight pounds. Now she has the amber eyes of a wolf and weighs sixty-four, more when we give her too many table scraps, but we're trying to cut back.

Soon, we'll be bringing her with us to France for six months, where the pâté and Camembert could shorten her life or at least make it harder for her to leap up on our bed to bid us a good morning. Until then, we're savoring the last of this North Country summer, which Zoë, with her luxurious black, wavy coat, has enjoyed more than usual because the temperature has rarely climbed above seventy degrees. Today, though, it's supposed to hit nearly eighty; we'll have to keep her in the shade. But because the Adirondack Museum is hosting a festival called Dog Days of Summer, she'll be with us all day. She's not allowed in the exhibits, but Kerry and I can take turns sitting with her under a tree while the other admires the maps and paintings of the Adirondacks done by the first surveyors. If those intrepid European-American adventurers could row across deep lakes and bushwhack primeval forests and ascend impossible peaks to map out the region, we can take our North Country dog for another kind of terrain-testing. In the past, we've brought Zoë along on a few vacations, but never to a place where dogs are the stars of the show, the reason for leaving home in the first place. So today's outing will be an adventure for all three of us, not just my husband and me.

Today's outing is also an experiment. Generally, when we see another dog on our walks, Zoë insists on a meet-and-greet. If she's off the lead, she's there before we know where *there* is. "She's friendly," we call while the blur of black and white charges off. Usually Zoë is made welcome, but sometimes the person with the dog warns, "My dog isn't nice to other dogs." If Zoë's on the lead when another dog comes into view, we're a shoulder strain or rotator cuff tear waiting to happen.

So how will she behave in dog-friendly France, where dogs are everywhere: under restaurant tables, on the bus, in the bar, at the bank, in the hotel lobby? From what I've gleaned through my travels, it would appear that all French dogs sit docilely at the feet of their people, seen but not heard; they don't charge across the restaurant floor to sniff another dog's butt, let alone provoke a poodle into a game of tackle, using, say, a dinner roll as the ball. They don't herd the dogs entering the restaurant or guard the door as other dogs leave, staging a body block. How will Zoë, who has done all of the above in our home in Canton, New York, fare in a culture of *politesse?*

Perhaps our French will get better, given all the apologies we'll be making, or maybe we'll make friends by setting up bilingual doggy play dates, and Zoë will not only rise to the occasion but will also become the American canine ambassador to Normandy. Our friends like to joke that she'll come back with an accent and a beret, but the truth is that Zoë is a dog who likes her routines, and because changes to her routine make her anxious, going to France will be hard on her, at least in the beginning, and I feel guilty about that. And she loves where we live, perhaps even more than *we* do. She loves the Grass River, the woods near our house, the long months of deep snow, the quiet, the piles of leaves in the yard to roll in and the space—especially the space. Zoë may have a deep need to greet other dogs when we're out in the world, but at home, she's a watch dog. If one trolls across the river within sight of her spot on the deck or deigns to pass the house, she barks and barks. *I'm* the designated dog here, she seems to be saying. Who invited you? She is not used to being in crowds or on city streets. A North Country dog spends a lot of time on dirt paths and fields and generally has access to lawns. A North Country dog doesn't have to turn a public sidewalk into her toilet, like the dogs in Rouen do, as I saw on my recent trip there, when I almost ruined a new pair of shoes.

But of course there *are* North Country dogs that relieve themselves on the sidewalk, or in this case, the paved walkway leading from the gift shop on the Adirondack Museum's grounds to the area that has been set up with an agility course. Kerry, Zoë and I arrive just in time to watch a young golden retriever leave a puddle at the feet of the woman petting him. The dog's human companion is a trim man with a silver military haircut and gun club T-shirt. Instantly, the man and I are commiserating about submissive peeing. "My dog used to do that," I say. "Especially around people she loved. You could say it's a compliment to the person she pees on."

"That's what I've been saying," he says, excited either to learn that his dog is not a freak or that we've found the same way to spin a nasty habit. "How did you get your dog to stop?"

"I think she just outgrew it," I say. "She did it until she was about a year and a half."

"Oh good," the man says. "We only have one month left." I think the conversation is over, but then he adds, "I haven't given her any water for a week, just to prepare for today, but it didn't work." He smiles, to let me know he's joking, that he's not really a sadist, that he loves his dog just as much as the rest of us here. I'm bad at counting, but Kerry thinks there are maybe one hundred dogs here strolling around with their people, leaving their marks on the grass or at the feet of their admirers.

Under normal circumstances, I would not strike up a conversation with a man in a gun shirt and a military haircut. But in Dog World, this man and I are comrades. We have something in common. Who knew?

When I started walking Zoë when she was a puppy, I found myself striking up conversations with people I would never, under any other circumstances, have reason to know. Most of those conversations have taken place on the campus of what used to be a two-year ag and tech school and is now part of the State University of New York. Canton doesn't have an official dog park, but SUNY Canton, with its wooded trails and expansive athletic fields, is an ideal place to let our dogs run off the lead, mostly because once we get to the fields and the woods we are away from the roads, safe from the danger of cars. Our makeshift dog park is far from perfect: sometimes we run into students who are afraid of our pets, or we encounter joggers and bicyclists who aren't thrilled when dogs jump on them or bark. There's also a lot of poison ivy growing along the river bank. But the trails are pretty—especially in May when the trillium comes out and in September and October when the oak and maple trees are ablaze and in winter when I make the trek in snowshoes—and conveniently close to home. Except for when we are away, Zoë comes here every single day, often twice. When we are back from a trip and we're done reacquainting ourselves with the house and yard, a walk over at SUNY Canton is the first thing she wants to do.

Kerry was a cat person when I met him; he was a reluctant convert to dogs. "Dogs need to be walked," he said. "They aren't as independent as cats." His wife had died the summer before I moved to town, and when he and I became friends, he was living in a house on the river with his two young sons and two male cats that would climb all over the counters and lap up the spilled milk and blotches of jam from breakfast. I fell in love with all of them—Kerry, the boys, the river, the house (which is my home now too) and the cats—but of the latter, Arnold and Bear, it was really Bear, the big, black, dog-like feline who prowled the yard possessively, ate our garden cucumbers and potatoes and licked our hair, who won my heart. Cats make me wheeze, but Bear was worth it. He was a magnificent animal: proud, dignified, loving and curious, and I still dream about him.

I think it's fair to say that Bear was also the prototype for Zoë. When I picked Zoë out at the pound, I knew Kerry would fall in love with her in part because of her resemblance to that cat.

Zoë was not, temperamentally, the puppy most people would have chosen. She was the only one in the litter of eight who did not trot over to say hello; she did not, like her siblings, climb all over me proffering kisses or roll on her back, inviting me to scratch her belly. She was the reserved, independent pup who sat on her own in the corner with one paw bent, gazing out calmly on all the commotion. The contemplative pup. The philosopher/poet. A sphinx, really. The dog that seemed cat-like and self-contained, who knew from the get-go how to entertain herself by sitting quietly, watching the world go by. I know it's not a good thing to anthropomorphize our pets, to project our emotions and desires onto them, let alone dress them up like elves or reindeer for Christmas cards as one of our neighbors does (Kerry lives in mortal fear that I will resort to these antics someday) or garland them with skirts like you'd wear to a luau and dance with them in a big grass pen while strangers watch (a treat that awaits us today on Dog Day, after lunch), but I do think anyone who has raised a dog will agree that each one is born with a distinct personality that we can tamper with only so much. And so Zoë began her life as the one watching from the sidelines, which is one reason why we were so surprised to discover she would crave canine companionship enough to pull our arms out of their sockets or dart across traffic to get to her own kind.

Because Kerry hadn't wanted a dog as I had, I promised to assume all the responsibility. How many people over the centuries have made this same promise to their loved ones? Not just children, but husbands or wives? I would do all the heavy lifting when it came to housebreaking: taking her outside every hour, responding to middle-of-the-night whimpers, cleaning up after accidents and picking up after her in the yard. I would enroll her in obedience classes; I'd pay for all the food and medicine; and above all, I would take her on her two or three daily walks.

Which is how, a few weeks after I brought Zoë home, I found myself hopping into the back of a silver SUV with a biologist from our campus, David, and his golden retriever, Maya, at 7:00 a.m. As soon as she jumped in, Zoë climbed onto the front seat's divider to lick David's ears.

And so our morning ritual began. Until now I'd spoken to David only at parties thrown by mutual friends, maybe once or twice a year, but now we were spending an hour together every morning, seven days a week, more time than I spend with my dearest, closest friends.

What I liked about those early walks through the SUNY Canton fields is how anyone out with a dog might spontaneously join us, how two pups playing and practicing their "come," "stay" and "sit" commands might suddenly become a pack of four, even six. And I enjoyed our rambling, chaotic discussions, interrupted as they were by canine action and the accordant human responses to canine action, such as "Leave it!" or "No!" or "Bring it back!" and, to the jogger/bicyclist groundskeeper running or wheeling past: "Sorry!" In our herky-jerky conversations we might start with the usual—tips on housebreaking, dog food brands, flea and tick medicine, treats—but soon we'd veer off, like pups chasing each other in a crazy loop, to childhood memories, religion, medicine, politics, travels, favorite books and David's search for the perfect turquoise earrings for his wife, Susan's, birthday.

On those early morning walks, David was equal parts jokester and ethicist, a seriously funny man, and vice versa. Every morning he'd have a brand-new off-color joke to test on me for its sexist content, and then we'd move on to his main agenda: the thorny medical ethical questions he'd be asking his students to debate that day in class. I learned I would need extra coffee before those walks to deconstruct his wit with wit and also to prevent myself, in an addled, emotional state, from offering a complete stranger a kidney.

Maya and Zoë became best friends. Their conversations were less complex than ours. They'd run together, jump in the water, carry out the same stick and then ignore each other for long stretches in a peaceable way when they found separate things to taste and smell.

On some mornings, Anita would join us with Cheyenne, the golden retriever she had rescued from a pound somewhere downstate. This dog had been rejected by five families and was deemed a lost cause by the time

Anita took her home. By then Cheyenne was two, but with the mentality and manners of a two-month old. If she'd been a child, Cheyenne would have been diagnosed with ADHD and doped up with Ritalin. At first, the dog was so excited to have someone new to play with that she would knock Anita down and chew on her arms and legs the way puppies gnaw on the limbs of their litter mates. Anita soon resembled the battered wife in *The Burning Bed,* as played by the late Farrah Fawcett; her friends and colleagues were concerned. But Anita was a special education teacher and was constitutionally incapable of giving up on anyone. She was also, I soon learned, a strict Catholic and a registered Republican, the only Republican I spoke to on a near-daily basis then, as the election of 2004 was heating up and I woke up each morning filled with dread and helpless rage. There were certain topics she and I instinctively stayed away from—abortion, for one— but I was surprised to discover how much we agreed on: that education was underfunded in the United States, that the gap between rich and poor had become grotesque and that the world would be a better place if dogs were welcome everywhere, including restaurants and museums.

That summer and fall, another woman I'll call Jill joined the mix, a history professor at a neighboring college. Her rescue dog did not play well with others, but we were happy to try to socialize her with our own less-than-perfect pups. On walks with Jill, the conversation veered more toward literature and social justice. Her transgendered partner's struggles to come to terms, her conservative parents' potential rejection of Jill if her partner became female: these were serious conversations for 7:00 in the morning, and we were honored to be sounding boards as we added another human and pup to our pack.

And so here we were—Catholic Republican special ed teacher, male biology professor with ethical riddles and jokes of questionable taste, fraught partner of transgendered social worker and me, a secular Jew who had marched against the war before it started and was wishing she could move to Canada, if not France—all talking about everything and nothing on a warm September morning, while our dogs ran free.

Eventually, Jill stopped coming because her dog acted out her fear/ aggression and tore Maya's ear so badly she needed stitches. And by the end of the fall, Anita would move to Nevada. Then, in February, I contracted pneumonia, probably from inhaling too many ice particles in the thirty-below-zero air of a typical North Country winter. My doctor prescribed bed rest, so Kerry took over the walks. By the time I was ready to resume my old routines, he asked if he could carry on doing the one in the morning, which he'd grown to love. Only now the A.M. amble/joke fest/ethical debate was called the Gentlemen's Walk. Although it had started as David and me, then David, me and two other women, those two women had, over time, been replaced by two men and their male dogs, a beagle and a Portuguese water spaniel. Kerry was the fourth man. The only creatures that had remained of the original pack were David, his Maya and our Zoë. Zoë was barely a year old and she had already parted company with four "friends," but the changes had been so gradual, she'd hardly seemed to notice.

In Dog World, we often encounter the same people and their dogs seven days a week (or dogs and their people, for often we will know the dogs' names and not the humans') and this continuity tricks us into thinking that things are stable in our lives, that nothing will ever change, that life will go on and on pretty much as it has before. But one day one of us will die, like our friend Neal's dog, Jasper, who sometimes visited Zoë on weekend afternoons to romp around our backyard. And until the big losses hit, canine or human, we rehearse them in small ways all the time without knowing we are doing it. Someone will decide to leave the group because her dog does not play well with others; someone will move to Nevada; or someone, like the man with the Portuguese water spaniel, will liquidate all his assets, buy gold and escape to Canada and the Cayman Islands just in time for the global recession. But each day we grab on to what we know just as our dogs do, basking in the familiar.

What amazes me as each group morphs into something else over time is how the dogs adjust to associating with dogs of other breeds and romping styles, just as some of us humans have to adjust to humans of different creeds. The beagles become more like retrievers, chasing sticks and learning to swim, and the sheepdog learns to hunt. Do these dogs really love each other, like we want to think they do? Or do they see each other as competition? Or both? Is it their distinct personalities, the ones they were born with, or their breeds that make them compatible or not?

Today, at Dog Day, people are wearing their love for their dog (and the dog's breed) on their sleeves, or at least their T-shirts. Over the span of the day we see a cocker spaniel T, a collie, a golden retriever, a black lab, a beagle. I won't buy a T-shirt with Zoë on it, I swear, but I do have a postage stamp with her puppy photo on it—a gift from my sister, another dog-lover, that was only partly done in jest.

One woman's T-shirt says, "All my children have paws."

At the museum's agility show, I'm moved by the woman in a walker who leads her four-year-old rescue mutt through all the jumps, balance beams, tunnels and weaving posts. There's a good variety of dogs here, mixes and pedigrees including breeds you wouldn't expect to see outside a standard show ring, like shih tzus, toy poodles and schnauzers, but overall it appears that herding dogs rule the agility world: shelties above all, followed by blue heelers and border collies. Zoë, whose Aussie/collie genes make her a natural herder, loved the agility class I took her to as a puppy, and I wish we'd had time to keep it up. Maybe she'd be up there now, weaving through those poles, flying through a tunnel?

I listen to the names of these nimble dogs: Pippin, Piggy, Magic, Tinkerbelle. Do dogs become the names we give them? A colleague's young daughter, who loves mythology, told me when she met Zoë as a pup that Zoë is Greek for bringer-of-life. I know that Zoë has brought Kerry and me a new reason to get out of bed each morning. There's the practical one, of course—she needs to go, *now*—but then there's the way a dog helps us see the world from dog-eye level. It begins with us being vigilant for hazards: will Zoë run into the road, or chase that squirrel, or jump on that bicyclist, or eat that bunny, live? But it also starts with that bonding when we and our pups imprint ourselves on each other in those first few weeks of our shared life, learning a common language: the human words for "sit," "stay," "come" and "treat." Our furry life-bringer gives us a glimmer of what it means to live fully, in the present tense, in a continuous stream of leaves fluttering in wind, sticks flying past, water flowing, birds hopping from branch to branch, clouds changing shape, day becoming night becoming morning again.

A friend of mine, a dog-lover from way back, once confessed to me that before she was medicated for depression she seriously considered suicide. What stopped her were her two toy poodles. No matter how bad things got, she knew she couldn't abandon those two, the two great loves of her life. But sometimes despair is a dark tunnel that takes us to one side of the world we can't return from, like those little culverts Zoë likes to run through at SUNY Canton that are so narrow I worry she'll never be able to turn around and come back. One bleak winter afternoon a few years ago, a woman in our village walked with her dog onto the wooded island at SUNY Canton, sat beneath a hemlock tree in the snow and put a plastic bag over her head. An hour later, when I went to walk my dog there, the bridge to the island was closed off with yellow police tape. This tragedy shook our small community in all the ways one would expect it to. Everyone was stricken that this smart, vibrant, loving mother, friend, and wife fell into a despair so deep that no one could get a lifeline around her that would carry her back home. But the horrible image I could not get out of my head was of her dog, a yellow lab mix, witnessing her person's death, then running back and forth frantically through the trees, trying to find someone to tell, someone to help her now that her human anchor to this earth had left the world and all her burdens behind.

We are often told that women in their fifties, as this woman was, are more prone to anxiety and depression, especially as they go through menopause. I am in this demographic now, and it is true that there were days, the year I turned fifty, when all I wanted to do was curl up next to Zoë and sleep right on the hard pine floor. I think about this season of dark weather during the Dancing with Dogs show after lunch, because all the humans (nine) are female and all but one, I'm guessing from their appearance, are post-menopausal. Is there something about this phase of life, when giving birth is no longer possible, that makes some of us all that more susceptible to a dog's charms? Is there a phase when canine companionship becomes more satisfying than, say, marriage? "My husband is my life partner, but my dog is my soulmate," an acquaintance of mine once said, when extolling the virtues of her Tibetan terrier.

Dogs have thrived because of the way they have adapted themselves to please humans; their survival depends on us loving and caring for them. But sometimes I think we need them far more than they need us. I think of all the hours these nine women have spent rehearsing together through the summer months just to prepare for this day. How many of them are buoyed up by their love of their dogs, held aloft like someone swimming in rough surf with a lifeline around her waist, being pulled to shore? How many of these women are widows? Do the dogs sleep beside them in their beds, claiming a side of the mattress for themselves, a pillow indented where a man's head once lay?

As the women twirl their canine partners to "The Mexican Hat Dance," Kerry takes a dozen pictures, but the bright red bandanas the women wear, and the matching shredded cloth colors the dogs wear like grass skirts around their necks, will not look nearly as bold against the blue sky in the pictures as they do in real life. And in writing about them, I'll alter the memory, as writing does to any experience. And here's the thing: while I'm laughing at the spectacle of aging women twirling their dogs to "The Mexican Hat Dance" in Blue Mountain Lake, New York, utterly aghast at the indignity of beloved pets performing as circus clowns, I also feel a kinship with all of them—dancing dogs, dancing women. And here's the other thing that surprises me: Zoë, for whose benefit we are supposedly here, looks bored. It's clear to us that she's totally done with the Dog Days of Summer at the Adirondack Museum. She wants to go.

So far the day has unfolded without mishap, but now, just before the women take a bow, I put Zoë's lead around a post of the fence barricading us from the dancers so that Kerry won't have to hold onto her while he takes pictures and I can visit with some cute boxer puppies a few yards over. Before I know what has happened, Zoë has pulled down our part of the fence and actually torn the plastic flap holding it in its post. "She was trying to get to you, not the other dogs," Kerry says. A man with a badge has to come over and repair the fence; he's nice, but I feel awful about it. But in this moment I realize something about Dog World and Zoë's place in it. When dogs are everywhere, even the stars of the show, Zoë takes them for granted. When they're no big deal to everyone else, they're no big deal to her either. She has passed the essential test that will gain her admission to the public spaces of France. All day long, until now, she has sat quietly at our feet. When Kerry and I took turns to go into each indoor exhibit, she waited calmly for the other to return. She has wagged her tail and offered her doggy grin to a few people and dogs, she has had her butt sniffed and she hasn't barked once. Overall, with the one exception when she tore the fence apart, she has been a model citizen. Doesn't she—don't we—deserve a sweet reward?

Afterward, we drive to Lake Placid to eat on the deck of Lisa G's, a wonderful restaurant whose owner loves and welcomes dogs. We're sitting down to giant plates of duck and preserved lemon on pasta (me) and halibut under green pepper coulis (Kerry), and Zoë's inclination is to form herself into a canine crescent, to take up as little space as possible beside us.

A woman passes our table. "Your dog looks just like mine. They could be litter mates!" We chat a little about our dogs and their histories, how we rescued them from pounds, Zoë from nearby Potsdam when she was a puppy, hers from Virginia when the dog was grown. "I'm going to take my dog out of the car and bring her to our table," she says, pointing up the stairs toward the upper level of the deck. "But unfortunately, she wasn't socialized well, and she hates other dogs. Would you mind distracting your dog, and sort of keep her out of the way, so that mine doesn't notice her?"

It's easy to lure Zoë to the other table legs with a chunk of duck, and the woman and her black dog walk past. The dog does not look at all like Zoë. She looks like a black lab with a bit of collie in her, does not have Zoë's high haunches or white belly and does not have her wolfy face, but she's just as pretty. And Zoë doesn't seem to notice her, or at least to let on that she does. Or maybe she just wants to please us, to communicate that our human companionship (and delicious table scraps) are enough, at least for now. This dog is ready for the bistros of France.

We drive home in early evening, content for our own separate reasons. It's still light out, and the sky is clear, the air warm but not hot. Zoë naps in the back seat, occasionally waking to look out the window at the blur of trees and lakes and street signs flying past. There's always a moment when we get closer to home that I can see her sitting up and peering out with her steady gaze, gladly taking in a landscape that is as familiar and essential to her, by smell and by sight, as it is to her human family. She knows when we're almost there.

If living with and walking a dog ties us to humans we might never have occasion to know, taking care of a dog also makes us mindful of the things we do every day. Dogs tie us to the quotidian, to the daily rituals that tie us to the Earth. They remind us of the animal in us, the creature that feels longing, attachment, loyalty, fierceness, hunger and love; that we are bodies coexisting on one Earth and that our bodies will one day grow old and die. And dogs tie us to a place: to a wider region, like the North Country, or more specifically, our backyard, or a favorite trail along the river through trees that becomes storied over time.

Today, at the museum, I thought about how a landscape becomes layered with human narrative. How the high peaks of the Adirondacks were made legend by the first European Americans who climbed them, and how a major event in history, say, the death of President McKinley that made Theodore Roosevelt president during his ascent of Mount Marcy, can turn a setting into a character in its own right. Maybe the frontier was closing, but those paintings and photographs by Thomas Cole and Seneca Ray Stoddard encoded the landscape we've just driven through with optimism: America, to the wild north, was still free, sublime and picturesque, a place where we could become our best selves.

Our local landscapes that we visit repeatedly with our dogs become encoded with stories as well, stories of danger, sorrow and pure joy. Behind that Scotch pine is where Zoë found the deer leg. That island over there, where our dogs chase each other to the water, is where two of us got poison ivy. That rock in the river that flows behind our house is where Kerry and I sat when we taught Zoë to swim by calling her to us, knowing our puppy's dread of being left behind was stronger than her fear of water. That bit of woods leading to Stillman Drive is where a woman killed herself with her dog at her side. It's also where Zoë met Cooper, her springer spaniel buddy. That boggy bit of river is where Cooper jumped in one winter and broke through the ice, and where he and his person, Pat, who crawled out after him, could have drowned if Kerry hadn't been there with a long branch to pull them out. That area that floods each year, that Pat and I nicknamed Land of the Lakes, is where Zoë caught a grouse. And that part of the path where the trillium blooms in May is where Pat always says, "Don't you think that we're incredibly lucky to be able to live here and to walk through woods like this with our dogs every day of our lives?"

THE ART OF AMISH GARDENING

By Betsy Tisdale

Edie — Hope you enjoy this! Betsy Tisdale

All names have been changed to protect the privacy that the Amish so highly prize.

If I told any of my Amish friends that their gardens are works of art, they would probably respond with puzzled expressions. They are not painters or sculptors or potters or writers or photographers or graphic designers—they are farmers.

They grow almost all the food they eat. Starting in early March, women and teenage girls spend many long hours raising seedlings in window greenhouses constructed by the men or an entire front porch or back porch enclosed in plastic. Or even free-standing homemade greenhouses with woodstoves to supply plants for a market garden.

The extremely conservative Swartzentruber Amish started moving here in 1974 from overcrowded eastern Ohio. St. Lawrence County is big and cold and remote, tucked up along the St. Lawrence River, which doubles as the Canadian border. A nasty and persistent wind blows across Canada from the north and west, riding above the wide St. Lawrence River sweeping our big, gently rolling land until fifty miles later fading out at the foothills of the Adirondacks. I've lived in Chicago, the so-called Windy City, and St. Lawrence County has far more wind. It starts snowing at the end of October and sometimes it has snowed on and even after Mother's Day in May, filling the ornamental pear blossoms of Potsdam street trees with wet snow, transforming the fragrant cups of pink blooms into cotton bolls. A ninety-day growing season tests the mettle of anyone trying to grow anything here to eat, much less sell the extra to help pay our high taxes. The soil is glacial till. No doubt about it, this is a tough place.

My own first vegetable garden was on an east-facing slope five hundred feet from Lake Champlain. My husband was just back from Vietnam. He was very silent and startled when bombers from Plattsburgh Air Force Base broke the sound barrier over us on training flights. He wouldn't go to parades or parties or church or anyplace with more than a few people. We were twenty-four and twenty-five years old. He had grown up in West Virginia. His mother had grown up gardening in a coal-mining town on the Monongahela River south of Pittsburgh. He knew the whole intricate process of vegetable gardening from A to Z. For me, it was a very steep learning curve.

We fought groundhogs, raccoons and deer. I picked and pulled and cleaned and shelled and cut up and froze peas, beans, chard, tomatoes, carrots, parsnips, zucchini, yellow squash, acorn squash, corn, potatoes, parsley, basil and dill. I sold canners full of fresh-picked and washed medleys of lettuce to a stingy restaurant owner for three dollars a canner. I sold tomatoes, beans and corn to summer people, calling for orders in the morning, delivering camp to camp in late afternoon. Many years later, some of these people told me our corn was the best they had ever eaten. We grew five kinds. We composted all our food scraps over the winter by simply dumping the bucket over a different part of the garden every week, then my husband would dig it all under in the early spring when the frost was gone. I remember watching little yellow boats of grapefruit rinds sliding across the snowy, icy crust in February.

But the Champlain Valley is still kinder and gentler than the glacial shield of the colder, windier St. Lawrence Valley more than one hundred miles to the west. The Amish have their work cut out for them.

Always optimistically buying run-down, exhausted farms, the Amish are masterful at building up the soil. Cow manure, horse manure, pig manure, chicken manure—soil replenishers all. Compost is a gardener's best friend, and the Amish are adept at turning it all into the black gold that produces delectable sweet red strawberries; jewel-like red and purple raspberries; many kinds of leaf lettuce and head lettuce; crunchy big red and white radishes; slender, snappy scallions; peas that are green candy in your mouth.

At my favorite roadside stand, near Kendrew Corners, the head lettuce sits crispy and gleaming in a dishpan with a few inches of cold well water. The children have peeled the outer layers off the onions. The little baby deep green zucchinis and curving yellow squash are lined up shining against the clean white oilcloth spread across the counter. Fresh-picked peas are bulging in their succulent pods. Baby carrots in small rubber-banded bunches have also been scrubbed by the children, like little orange groups of fallen soldiers.

I glance up and over to one of the quarter-acre gardens on either side of the stand and see the bearded father with a straw hat patiently guiding his workhorse through another long row of bush beans, sitting behind his cultivator. Successive plantings of many vegetables yield a month or two of some vegetables instead of a few weeks.

"The corn is coming along good. If things go right, maybe we'll have some for you next week."

Sarah is always pleasant to me. I like to listen to her world. Winter is when we are all cooped up in our houses. Summer is when we are outside again, happy, able to visit each other at the stand. But Sarah and her husband, teenage daughters and sons are BUSY in capital letters. Her oldest children are married and gone, some in other states. Her youngest, a boy, is severely handicapped, unable to walk and requires a lot of care. He is a "special" child, and they all lavish him with love and attention. He yells and waves to me from his wheelchair on the porch. I wave back and walk over to talk with him. I'm getting better at understanding his garbled speech, and he likes my teasing and any silly sense of humor I can muster.

One day when he was about eight years old, I brought him a "Magic" erasable sketchboard with a red plastic stylus. It was a happy reminder of my 1950s childhood.

Henry was thrilled. His thick golden hair, glinting in the sun, tumbled in front of his face as he bent over this strange present. Between customers his mother carefully showed him how to press down with the stylus on the clear plastic page and thinner dark gray carbon sheet underneath. Sarah guided Henry's hand to write, "Thank you, Betsy." His tendons and muscles contort his crippled fingers. Braces are clamped onto his legs. Blue eyes shining, he lifts his Magic Easel in joy for my approval. Laundry flaps on the line behind us. The house is startlingly white in the sun. Even, orderly rows of vegetables march in dark rich soil on each side of us. A group of horses are lazily grazing in a pasture downhill.

"Thank you, Betsy," Henry says, barely intelligible. He and his mother are grinning at me. Such a simple thing. So much gratitude.

"You're welcome, Henry." I am overwhelmed. I walk back to my car in front of the stand, drive down the road and start crying.

Six miles later at another stand, Amanda greets me warmly. This family has a lot of girls who help their mother in the gardens and at the stand.

One family might have carrots before the others or offer a second planting of green beans and wax beans. One might offer Flavor Keeper cabbage, tight-packed, sweet, long-lasting. One family might have Bodacious corn, another Lancelot, another Incredible. I guess correctly they might not know the meanings of these words since their English vocabulary is small. They admit they don't know, so I explain and their eyes light up. But Lancelot is difficult. The concept of a knight in shining armor is something far beyond their imagination. The Amish are pacifists. Their sons do not go to war. Stories about war are not permitted reading matter for their children.

At another farm, I fill my car trunk with an order of forty quarts of dazzling red Honeoye strawberries. Two lovely teenage girls help me carefully fill the trunk. Then we fill the backseat and floor with more quart boxes of ruby red treasure. Their little brothers stare hard into the trunk and backseat of my capacious gray Buick. Boys are always interested in cars or trucks. Always watching, listening. I ask if they would like to close the trunk and car doors. Big grins. But first I show them how not to smash their fingers. They slam closed the trunk lid and car doors with careful joy.

Amish children are generally strong and obedient and enjoy being "useful." These children (seventeen in this family) have been up since dawn picking strawberries. They are barefoot with tanned arms and faces. Long dark pants, blue shirts, black suspenders on the boys. White caps and blue, purple, black, brown or green dresses with aprons on the girls. They've been out of school since the first week of May and will return to their one-room schoolhouse in early September, with time off in late fall for feed corn husking.

Rows of onions, beans, potatoes, carrots, cabbages, raspberries, peppers, tomatoes, melons, acorn squash, butternut squash, Hubbard squash and watermelons run downslope from the front yard to the road and beyond along the south side of the house. The size of it all staggers me.

Emma, the mother, invites me up into the cool shade of the porch for a drink of water. A ten-year-old girl shyly hands me the clear plastic cup.

"We're growing for the Farm to Table program this year," says Emma, brushing a wisp of blonde hair off her sweaty forehead. She is still pretty with clear light blue eyes after seventeen children.

"It's a lot of work," she says, an obvious and typical understatement. We look out together from the shady porch at what I consider a living painting. Fields and woods across the road dip down to Fish Creek. Swallows swoop in and out of the barn, careening over the gardens, catching flies and mosquitoes.

A man in a broken-down pickup truck pulls up to an old door-less refrigerator at the end of the lane, removes two quarts of strawberries, hands them to his wife in the truck and leaves money in a slotted metal box attached to the side of the refrigerator. Then he glances uphill to the porch and waves. Emma waves back. He drives away.

"That's our neighbor," Emma says simply.

The windmill near the barn creaks and squeaks as it turns in a light breeze. "Feels good to have that air moving across my face," says Emma.

Behind us through the open screened windows of the kitchen, her four teenage daughters are setting the long, white oil cloth-covered table for nineteen—a knife, fork and spoon thrown noisily into a stainless steel bowl in front of an opaque plastic cup at each place. A bowl of homemade bright yellow butter, two loaves of fresh warm bread just out of the woodstove oven, a bowl of fresh strawberry jam...I can hear and smell beef (home-grown, of course) sizzling in several enormous cast iron skillets, with onions.

"Would you like to stay for dinner? We're having strawberry shortcake for dessert," she adds with a bashful smile.

"Well, I guess my neighbors can wait a little while longer for their strawberries," I answer with a grin. Dinner for twenty!

"We have some extra beans, I think; would you like some?"

"Yes, I would."

She turns and says something in German to two little boys resting in the shade of a tree at the end of the porch. One grabs a bucket, and they go racing into rows of bush beans.

Emma turns back to me from watching the boys. "Well, I guess they still have a little energy to pick a few beans," she offers with a tired smile. She always wants to give me something.

Many of my Amish friends do this too—a jar of homegrown Thumbelina popcorn, a zip-lock sandwich bag of hulled and dried and picked black walnuts, a loaf of bread warm from the oven ("there is some of our own wheat in it"), a pint of ruby red seedless raspberry jam ("I put them through a sieve and used a big spoon back and forth across"). Or a jar of homemade condensed tomato soup ("this will make enough for sixteen people"), a big bunch of luscious dark green curly parsley cut with a big knife from a twelve-foot row.

A girl walks to the garden with a knife and big plastic grocery bag. "How many beets would you like?" These are the columnar beets, the really sweet tender ones. Her hands and wrists and forearms are strong and tan and sinewy at sixteen. I have never seen an anorexic Amish teenager.

But there are frail, pale Amish children and teenagers with cystic fibrosis, common in this group. The strong help the weak.

One day I arrived at a farm where the couple had nineteen children. Naomi, the mother, was whaling away with a hoe digging a straight furrow in the garden, very fast. She was swinging the hoe way up over her head and bringing it down in a vicious arc to the ground.

"I can't stop now. My sweet potatoes just came in the mail. I've got to get them into the ground."

I stood watching at a safe distance and realized that I would not want to be in the way of the sharp blade of her hoe.

"Go along inside and talk with my husband. I'll come in when I get this done."

May through September, there is not a moment to lose. Gardening and canning are serious business. Then after canning jars are all neatly arranged on shelves in the cellar, it is slaughtering time: chickens, then a pig or two, then a beef cow…and more canning of the meat. Some of the men go deer hunting, so venison goes into jars as well.

Another day I was sitting in the cool kitchen in an old farmhouse talking with one of the quilters I worked with during more than twenty years as a quilt dealer and designer when her husband, maybe thirty-two, came running full-speed in the back door, grabbed a big coffee can off the kitchen table between Elizabeth and me, turned, ran (barefoot) out the back door and jumped off the back porch.

I looked at Elizabeth, who had not moved a muscle or changed her serene expression and asked, "What was that about?"

"Oh, he's hitched up the horses, and he's ready to plant corn. That's what was in the coffee can."

Last December, Emma told me, "$1,000 worth of butternut squash rotted. We kept hoping Sue (the buyer and coordinator for the Farm to Table program) would be able to find a buyer. She always had before. But not even the Food Bank wanted it."

I studied her face as she fell silent and then looked out the window. That was $1,000 they really needed—for taxes, to help a son soon to be married. She said nothing, but I was trying silently to fill in the blanks as I drove the forty miles home in a car redolent with strawberries.

I knew that the year before $5,000 of strawberry money had been stolen from a hidden compartment in their dresser drawer while the family was at church. Her husband had planned to deposit the money in the bank in Heuvelton ten miles away the next morning. But summer is so busy. He and his sons had been haying and working in the gardens, milking the cows, feeding the animals...it takes half a day by horse and buggy for a round trip to Heuvelton.

I learned about the stolen money from another Amish couple, not from Emma and Joe. When Emma told me about the rotten squash, she looked tired and discouraged. I didn't know what to say.

Once again, thinking of these industrious Amish gardeners, I thought how good it might be to have a canning and freezing plant inside the big, new, empty anonymous building sitting in a former farm field a half mile from my house in Potsdam. The building was financed by taxpayers' money to spur economic development.

More Swartzentruber Amish families, mostly young, have been settling east of Potsdam all the way to the Franklin County line twenty miles away. One of those young Amish farmers passes my house twice every Saturday and Wednesday, his wagon filled with vegetables, his team of horses steadily clip-clopping the fifteen-mile round trip.

I wonder if surplus vegetables and berries grown by the Amish (and English, as they call us) could be delivered to a canning and freezing plant right here in St. Lawrence County. Then, maybe, less would be wasted. The food could be sold from Ogdensburg on the St. Lawrence River to Plattsburgh over one hundred miles east on Lake Champlain, from Massena to Tupper Lake. It would create more jobs, feed more people and help the county be more self-sufficient.

Heritage Cheese Plant in Heuvelton has closed. It was built and financed partly by the Amish so that they would have a market for their milk. The rumor is "mismanagement, graft and corruption" by the English management. Various kinds of Heritage Cheese, cheddar, Muenster and Monterey jack won blue ribbons at the state fair in Syracuse when the plant was managed by the first owners, a father-and-son team. Soon after they sold the plant, the boilers failed and had to be replaced. The Amish dug deep into their pockets to pay ahead for a Midwest company to fabricate the boilers. Months went by, and the Amish had to dump their milk during the wait for the boilers. There was no other market; only cheese can be made from hand-milked cows from farms without electric equipment and refrigeration. It was a hardship.

Finally, the new boilers arrived and were installed. The truck resumed picking up full milk cans at Amish farms. People were pleased to line up once again at Heritage Cheese on the west edge of Heuvelton for fresh warm cheese curds in the afternoon. It squeaks between your teeth as you gently chew the odd-shaped bite-sized pieces of light yellow curd, warm and salty in your mouth. It's a quick trip to heaven.

My son and I once ate a whole pound of fresh, warm jalapeno cheese curd from a clear plastic bag on the car seat between us during a drive home twenty-five miles from Heuvelton to Potsdam. There was nothing left when we pulled into our driveway. We had saved none to share with my husband, David. We were ashamed of ourselves. Plain cheese curd, chive cheese curd, bacon and horseradish cheese curd, clunky, warm, big and small pieces packed as you watch by a male or female worker wearing a white apron and hairnet—Heritage was the only cheese plant in the area selling cheese curd, to a very devoted and varied group of fans.

But still the Amish were not receiving milk checks. After six months, some started to sell their herds. Finally, Heritage Cheese mysteriously closed with no explanation. The Amish once again were between a rock and a hard place, as they are not allowed to own a retail business (too much exposure to the outside world). More families now are trying to sell eggs from their farms, furniture, cedar fence posts, home-baked bread, cookies and pies, baskets, quilts, aprons, garden sheds (and custom orders), maple syrup, vegetables, berries, fishing worms and firewood. Career choices are very limited for the Swartzentruber Amish.

"A gallon of wood ashes, a gallon of agricultural lime and a handful of sulfur. Mix it dry in a big bucket and hand-cast it at the base of your raspberry canes and fruit trees. It helps control the Japanese beetle grubs in the ground. We've had good luck with it."

Another of my quilters is giving me good advice on how to combat the Japanese beetles that have come north with global warming in the last three years and decimated my Martha Washington red raspberries. She and I have just picked two quarts of gorgeous ruby red raspberries from a big patch of healthy plants by the outhouse. Six years ago, I had dug up some of my raspberry shoots to give this young couple soon after they bought this tired-out farm. Now the place was verdant in their care. My own raspberries were not doing nearly as well.

After I had paid her for a quilt order and we stepped out of her cool, orderly kitchen onto the porch, she followed me to the car holding the two boxes of raspberries while I carried my purse and the quilt. We talked a few minutes in the welcome warm sun of late July after stowing berries on the car floor and the quilt on the back seat. I can't remember what prompted Elizabeth to say what she said next. But I do remember she looked steadily with her light blue eyes into my eyes, and blonde wisps of hair blew across her forehead, escaping from her white organdy cap.

"Having too much isn't good, and having too little isn't good. But having just enough is good."

I had never heard that before. As I backed out of the lane and started my long drive home on country roads on a beautiful mid-summer late afternoon, Amish men and boys waved to me from their hay wagons hitched up to matched pairs of Belgian and Percheron workhorses.

So, "Just enough is good." That is a lesson Elizabeth felt she needed to share with me. She is young enough to be my daughter. I am still trying to learn that simple and difficult dictum, at a comparatively late age.

Our ninety-day growing season forces North Country farmers and gardeners to work hard and fast when the time is right. In a long, wet spring, seeds rot in the ground and so planting needs a second round. If we have a wonderful, long, hot summer with enough rain at the right times, the Amish can barely keep up with the harvest.

"I don't like a bumper crop," exclaims Rachel to me, hot, sweaty and tired, plopping into a bentwood rocker in the living room to nurse a baby (her ninth) after helping her husband bring in the last load of hay with their teenage daughters. "We got it into the barn just before the storm," she adds with a great deal of relief and a little smile on her face.

"No, just enough is really better for me. A bumper crop just makes us all tired and then what should we do with so much extra?"

"Can't you sell the extra hay?"

"Probably not. It's a very good year, so everyone has extra."

I remain quiet to let her rest and nurse her baby. Besides, it's a beautiful rare summer day in St. Lawrence County. I look out her windows past the vegetable garden, the raspberries, the fruit trees and the hayfield to the blue sky and clouds to the west. Then the heavens quickly turn dark with fast-moving, roiling clouds charging in from Canada ten miles west across the St. Lawrence River. Suddenly, hard drops of rain are pelting the metal roof above us. Three quiet children play with blocks at my feet, two little boys and a girl, all dressed in clothes identical to those of their parents. The five older children are in the barn with their father, forking hay into the loft. I've come to pick up a finished quilt but am receiving so much more. Just enough for today.

Afterword

RIVERS

By Neal Burdick

By the banks of the sweet Saranac,
Where its limpid waters flow...
—from the Adirondack folk song
"Once More a'Lumbering Go"

In all the world there is only one river, and we are part of it. All water is the same, and the same water flows from clouds to brooks to ponds to rivers to oceans and back to clouds, falling on Earth, flowing, evaporating and falling on Earth again in the timeless hydrologic cycle: one river.

I grew up a short walk from where one vein of this universal river meets a lake. As a boy I would try to pin my eyes to a single patch of Saranac River water as it slid into voracious Lake Champlain and wonder where it had come from, and how long it had taken to reach me, and what happened to it as it melted before my eyes into the vastness of the lake. Someone, perhaps one of my parents, patiently explained that it came down from Saranac Lake, on the fringe of my childhood world of reference. Once I learned of the hydrologic cycle, though, I realized my patch of water was an assemblage of many parts that had come from much farther away and would pass by me again someday, and was comforted. And when finally I came to comprehend that we live out our own cycles, I saw that we are one with water.

I learned in school that our bodies are nearly two-thirds water. Each cell bears the chemistry, the memory, of water. As my cosmos expanded, I understood that we are more than merely physically akin to water. "My soul has grown deep like the rivers," wrote the poet Langston Hughes in "The Negro Speaks of Rivers." Geologists tell us that rivers are the prime shapers of Earth's surface; they are shapers of us as well. Trillions of gallons of water flow through all the channels of the world's one river at each moment—at this moment—but we can hold a drop on our fingertips. That drop is us.

As it tumbled from the Adirondack highlands to the Champlain Valley floor, the Saranac River of my youth may not have been sweet or limpid, subject as it was to farm runoff, logging debris, municipal waste and paper mill discharge, but it was and remains my natal water, and thus it remains part of me, and I of it. My first ventures from my home, three blocks from the river in downtown Plattsburgh, without the guidance of my mother's protecting hand, took me to the foot of a granite monument commemorating the American victory on land and lake over the British in September 1814. From there I could watch the river water glide reliably, satisfyingly toward the lake and wonder if the soldiers in that battle saw the same water that I did, perhaps the last thing some of them saw before they died.

The river flows under the D&H Railroad bridge moments before melding with the lake; trains would rumble over that bridge, long freights and shining passenger trains, and I would wonder what was in the boxcars and who was in the coaches and sleepers and the dining car, and where they had come from and where they were going, and why, and whether they were part of some great intangible cycle too. How long did they take to reach me, and would they pass by me again one day, here or somewhere else? Was I part of them, and they of me?

A friend, a biology professor with a streak of philosopher, says we must all seek the headwaters of the river nearest our home, nearest our roots, and follow that river to its conclusion, not in a car along convenient roads, separated from it, but on foot or in a vessel. We must become one with it. For only then will we begin to know where we have come from, and where we are going, and where we fit in the great cycle. My Saranac collects the fallen rains and snows of the northern Adirondacks and then carries them through forests, past hamlets, along farm fields and over dams, down into the Champlain Valley before blending them into Lake Champlain, where it rides the currents into the St. Lawrence River and on to the Atlantic Ocean before returning to the sky to carry the cycle on. This is who I am.

Heraclitus, the Greek philosopher, said, "You cannot step into the same river twice," meaning nothing stays the same. That may be true superficially, but the fundamental cycle continues, always in flux but in superficial ways. It is bigger than we are. We may never intercept it at the same point—I may never find that precise patch of water I fixed my eye on as a child—but it goes on nonetheless. That patch is somewhere in the cycle.

"We must begin thinking like a river if we are to leave a legacy of beauty and life for future generations," said the environmentalist David Brower. A Native American song puts it this way: "The rivers are our sisters, and we must take care of them." In thinking like a river, we reflect on our own lives, our own cycles. In taking care of rivers, we take care of ourselves.

It is our tendency to break the universal cycles (water, the stars, the seasons) into fragments and categorize and name the fragments, so that we lose consciousness of the cycles. "Saranac" means "Place of the red summer," in reference to sumacs, in Algonquian. Are there any sumacs left beside the sweet Saranac's limpid waters? If so, is it because we have taken care of the river? If not, what have we wrought?

In all the world, there is only one river. Water flows in an eternal cycle, and we are part of it. What we do to rivers, we do to ourselves.

Perhaps all of this is why rivers appear in so many of the selections in this anthology. We are part of them, and they of us. As the spiritual puts it, "Give us peace like a river."

ABOUT THE EDITORS

NEAL BURDICK grew up in Plattsburgh, New York, and graduated from St. Lawrence University, where he has been publications writer/editor and an advanced writing instructor since 1977. As a freelance editor and writer, he has published in a variety of genres, from poetry to book reviews, and in a variety of publications, from Fodor's Travel Books to *Blueline*. He even won a short fiction contest once, although he thinks he was the only entrant in his age category. He is editor of *Adirondac*, the magazine of the Adirondack Mountain Club, and a frequent contributor to *Adirondack Explorer* and *Adirondack Life* magazines. Burdick is co-editor,

Tara Freeman.

with Natalia Singer, of the anthology *Living North Country* (North Country Books, 2001) and editor of *The Adirondack Reader, 3rd Ed.* (Adirondack Mountain Club, 2009). He has edited books on the Adirondacks for several regional publishing houses; been a panelist for the New York Foundation for the Arts nonfiction grant program and a commentator on regional writing for the Associated Writing Programs, North Country Public Radio and the Adirondack Park Visitor Interpretive Center; and was for several years a member of the board of directors of the Adirondack Center for Writing. He was a founder and longtime co-director of St. Lawrence's Young Writers Conference.

The author of over thirty collections of poetry and fiction, Watertown, New York native MAURICE KENNY has been hailed by *World Literature Today* as the dean of Native American poetry. Also an essayist and reviewer, his work appears in nearly one hundred anthologies and textbooks. *The Mama Poems*, an extended elegy, won the American Book Award in 1984, and his books *Between Two Rivers, Blackrobe* and *Isaac Jogues* were nominated for the Pulitzer Prize. However, he considers his most important work to be *Tekonwatonti: Molly Brant, 1735–1795*, a historical poetry journey in many voices that was praised as "a new form of dramatic monologue." He has extended this method in the forthcoming *Conversations with Frida Kahlo: Collage of Memory.* Kenny has been an editor, publisher, arts council panelist and member of the board of directors of the Coordinating Council of Literary Magazines. He has been a visiting professor/poet-in-residence at numerous colleges, including St. Lawrence University, which awarded him an honorary doctorate; the University of Oklahoma; Paul Smith's College; and SUNY Potsdam, where he was writer-in-residence. He was for many years a teaching poet at St. Lawrence's Young Writers Conference.

Phil Gallos.

ABOUT OUR CONTRIBUTORS

CHRIS ANGUS'S articles and essays on the Adirondack region have appeared in many publications, including the *New York Times*, *Albany Times-Union*, *Adirondack Life*, *Canoe*, *Adirondac* and *American Forests*. His work also appears in a number of anthologies, including *Living North Country*, *Rooted in Rock* and *The Adirondack Reader*. He is the author of *Reflections From Canoe Country: Paddling the Waters of the Adirondacks and Canada* and *The Extraordinary Adirondack Journey of Clarence Petty: Wilderness Guide, Pilot and Conservationist*, both published by Syracuse University Press, and *Oswegatchie: A North Country River*, published by North Country Books. He has also written a number of historical thrillers, including *London Underground* and *The Last Titanic Story*, published by Iguana Books, and *Flypaper*, published by Cool Well Press. The books are available in print, e-book and audio editions from Amazon.

JOHN BERBRICH was born and raised on Long Island, New York. He has worked in factories, a car wash, food service and as a construction grunt; has played in several experimental rock bands; and is currently an obscure paperwork drudge in a dreary government office building. He and his wife, Nancy, are co-rulers of BoneWorld Publishing, under the aegis of which are published the literary quarterly *Barbaric Yawp* and the many chapbooks of MuscleHead Press. He also writes monthly music and literary review columns for *Fourth Coast Entertainment Magazine* and is a founding member of SLAP (St. Lawrence Area Poets). John and Nancy live among the northwestern foothills of the Adirondack Mountains in Russell, New York.

Born and raised in St. Lawrence County, NANCY BERBRICH has been co-editor and co-publisher of the literary quarterly *Barbaric Yawp* and for MuscleHead Press, the chapbook division of BoneWorld Publishing, for the several years. She is one of the founding members of SLAP (St. Lawrence Area Poets), writers who seek to support and promote poetry in the North Country. Her poems have been featured in numerous magazines. She's been a teacher in the English and Communication Department at SUNY Potsdam since 1996.

ROBERT L. CARDARELLI was born in 1934 in Rochester, New York. His high school years were spent in Elmira, New York, and from 1953 until 1957 he served in the U.S. Navy. His tour of duty took him to ports of call in the Mediterranean and Caribbean. After graduating from Ithaca College with a BA in English, he taught high school English in Rochester from 1961 to 1968. From 1964 until 1997, he was cofounder and president of Cardwell Construction Company, Inc. Shortly after his retirement in 1998, he took up permanent residence in Cape Vincent, New York, where he resides with Lilo, his wife of fifty-three years. A member of Poets and Writers, Ink., his love of language and fascination with the story continues.

VARICK CHITTENDEN is Professor Emeritus of Humanities at SUNY Canton, where he taught English, folklore and American rural studies. In 1986, he was the founding director of Traditional Arts in Upstate New York (TAUNY) and continues as director of special projects. His research interests include folk art, vernacular architecture, foodways and regional oral traditions. He has curated numerous exhibits, published in scholarly journals and popular magazines and produced several series of documentary features on regional folk culture for North Country Public Radio. A native of St. Lawrence County, he holds a BA and an MEd from St. Lawrence University and an MA in American folk culture from the Cooperstown Graduate Program of SUNY Oneonta.

PAUL GRAHAM teaches writing and literature at St. Lawrence University. His collection of short stories, *Crazy Season*, was published in 2012, and he was the recipient of the 2005 Dana Literary Award for the Novel. His essays have appeared widely, including in *The Best Food Writing 2012*.

RICK HENRY has published fiction and articles in a variety of journals and anthologies. His books include *Chant* (BlazeVox Books, 2008); *Lucy's Eggs and Other Stories* (Syracuse UP, 2006), winner of the 2006 Adirondack Center for Writing Literary Award for Best Work of Fiction; *Pretending and Meaning: Toward a Pragmatic Theory of Fictional Discourse*, a philosophical inquiry

(Greenwood Publishing, 1996); and *Sidewalk Portrait: Fifty-fourth Floor and Falling*, a novella (BlazeVox Books, 2006). In addition, he is co-editor of *The Blueline Anthology* (Syracuse University Press, 2004) and is a former editor of *Blueline*. He teaches at SUNY Potsdam.

HEATHER L. HORNING earned her master's degree at the University of Connecticut. She is also a SUNY Potsdam alumna, where her undergraduate degree is in English education. She also continues to entertain an interest in acting. Her future plans include teaching English abroad for a year or two.

BETSY KEPES grew up in Canton, New York, and explored the world before returning to the North Country with her husband, Tom Van de Water, to build a simple house in the hills of Pierrepont. A graduate of Williams College, she teaches piano to children and adults and accompanies students at the Crane School of Music, SUNY Potsdam. She is a freelance writer and the book reviewer for North Country Public Radio, and her work is included in the anthologies *Wild with Child* and *A Mile in Her Boots: Women Who Work in the Wild*. In the summer she and her family work clearing trails for the U.S. Forest Service in the Selway Bitterroot Wilderness in central Idaho.

GORDIE LITTLE planned to become a civil engineer, but radio turned out to be his true calling. After graduating with Stony Brook University's first class in 1961, he took his first commercial radio job in Plattsburgh, where he worked for almost thirty-six years. In 1997, he left that business to spend eight years as a crime victims' advocate and simultaneously began a writing career, penning regular newspaper and magazine columns and articles. He does weekly ninety-minute television documentaries and writes "true" ghost stories and children's books; his *Ghosts of Clinton County* was published by North Country Books in 2009, followed in 2011 by a children's book entitled *Little Champy Goes to School*. He and his wife, Kaye, love nature and live next to the picturesque Saranac River in Morrisonville, New York, where they've raised a large family.

North Country Public Radio station manager ELLEN ROCCO has been with the station since 1980. She has lived on her DeKalb, New York farm since 1971, when she moved to the North Country from New York City. Over the past four decades she has raised sheep, Percheron horses, chickens, turkeys and a son. She is the producer and host of the contemporary literature series *Readers & Writers on the Air*.

OSCAR D. SARMIENTO is professor in modern languages at SUNY Potsdam. His book *El otro Lihn: La práctica cultural de Enrique Lihn* was published by

University Press of America in 2001, and his articles on contemporary Latin American poetry have appeared in a number of scholarly journals. He is poetry editor for the Chilean poetry chapter of the *Handbook of Latin American Studies* of the Library of Congress and is also on the editorial board of *Blueline*, the regional literary magazine. His translations of poems by Brooklyn native Martín Espada were published as *La República de la Poesía* by Mago Editores in 2007, and his translations of poems by Philip Lopate, Kathleen Sheeder Bonano and Maurice Kenny can be found on the *Letras de Chile* literary website. His own poems have been published in a number of literary magazines and his book *Carta de Extranjería* was published by Asterión in 1992. He is the composer of some of the songs on the *El sur es mi norte*.

NATALIA RACHEL SINGER is a professor of English at St. Lawrence University, where she teaches courses in creative writing and environmental literature. She is the author of *Scraping by in the Big Eighties*, a memoir, and was co-editor with Neal Burdick of *Living North Country: Essays on People and Landscapes of Northern New York* (North Country Books, 2001). She is in the final stages of completing a novel, *The Inventions of Love*, and is working on a travel memoir set in France, India and the United States, *On Temple Road*. In addition, she has begun a memoir called *Winter with Zoë: On Love, Dogs, and Mortality*. A past winner of the Annie Dillard Award for Nonfiction and the World's Best Short Short Story Contest, she has published fiction and nonfiction in *Redbook, The North American Review, O: The Oprah Magazine, Harper's, The Writers' Chronicle, The Chronicle of Higher Education, Creative Nonfiction* and many other journals and magazines.

In the summer of 2011, Zoë was diagnosed with bone cancer. She passed away in July 2012. To read that story, and to see more photos of Zoë and her people, go to http://winterwithzoe.blogspot.com/.

Photographer and writer BETSY TISDALE's work has appeared in the Plattsburgh *Press Republican, Adirondack Life, The Conservationist* and *Adirondac* (the magazine of the Adirondack Mountain Club), and she contributed a chapter to the anthology *Living North Country: Essays on People and Landscapes of Northern New York* (North Country Books, 2001). A resident of Potsdam, New York, she was a quilt dealer and designer for more than twenty years, which led to some very rewarding friendships with her Swartzentruber Amish quilters and their families. She has taught English as a second language to adult students.

JILL VAUGHAN lives with her family on a farm in Moira, a few miles from the Quebec border in the St. Lawrence Valley. She's worked in human services for more than two decades and is a poet and writer. She's been a commentator for North Country Public Radio and National Public Radio and has been a resident at Blue Mountain Center.

ABOUT OUR ILLUSTRATORS

In addition to those named here, writers Varick Chittenden, Natalia Singer and Betsy Tisdale, whose biographies appear above, also contributed illustrations.

ANNA GERHARD ARNOLD'S watercolors focus on the ordinary images central to the rural North Country and the Adirondacks. She has completed more than a dozen illustration covers for the annual Lake Placid Horse Show, is featured in several POLO Magazine Sporting Art issues, has illustrated three books and contributes regularly to Art Show at the Dog Show in Wisconsin. She paints commissioned fine art portraits of dogs and horses while working out of her art studio on her windy hilltop Greythorne Farm in Waddington, New York. Her work can also be seen in murals, signage and interiors at businesses and universities in Canton and Potsdam.

JIM BULLARD is an artist/photographer living in the North Country of New York, north and west of the Adirondack Park. His photography consists primarily of landscapes and flowers. He has a blog at http://jims-ramblings. blogspot.com and photo galleries at http://jimbullard.zenfolio.com.

MARTHA COOPER is a Manhattan-based documentary photographer with an international reputation for her photographs of urban street art and folk culture of all kinds. The first of many books by her, *Subway Art*, first published in 1984, is widely recognized among street artists as the authoritative work on graffiti. Her work appears in *National Geographic*, *Smithsonian* and numerous other magazines. Since 1988, she has photographed for various projects for Traditional Arts in Upstate New York (TAUNY).

TARA FREEMAN has been the university photographer at St. Lawrence University since 2000. She has seventeen years of experience as a professional photographer. Before coming to St. Lawrence, she was a staff photographer at the *Olean Times Herald*, in Olean, New York.

WHIT HAYNES was a student assistant to the university photographer at St. Lawrence University before graduating in 2010 with a major in fine arts. A winner as an undergraduate of an acting award named for St. Lawrence alumnus Kirk Douglas, he lives in the Boston, Massachusetts area.

A 1970 graduate of Gloversville (New York) High School and a 1976 graduate of St. Lawrence University, BRIAN HENRY has had his bird photos published in, among others, *Adirondack Life, Birder's World, Bird Watcher's Digest, Time Magazine, WildBird* and many birding field guides. Retired from the New York State Thruway Authority/Canal Corporation, he works part-time as a health insurance navigator for the Family Counseling Center of Fulton County (New York), Inc.

Born in Chicago and raised in Connecticut, DEBBIE KANZE moved to Saranac Lake in the Adirondacks in 1999. A photographer by passion and avocation, she serves as activities director at Saranac Village at Will Rogers, a senior independent living residence in Saranac Lake. Nature, landscapes and intriguing patterns of light and shadow on water are favorite subjects for her camera.

JOHN LAFALCE is a native of Buffalo, New York, and graduated from Buffalo State University in 2002 with a BFA in painting. He was a member of the "Combat Paper Project" for many years. He is an adjunct instructor of art at North Country Community College and the studio technician for BluSeed Studios in Saranac Lake, New York.

DIANE LEIFHEIT works in pastel, making plein-air landscapes and portraits. Her award-winning work has been included in numerous solo and group exhibitions, both regionally and nationally, and has been published by North Light Books in *Strokes of Genius* and by Kennedy Publications in *Best of Pastel*. She has a studio in Gabriels, New York, in the north-central Adirondacks, where she offers small studio classes in drawing and pastel.

BARRY LOBDELL lives in Saranac Lake, in the heart of the Adirondack Park. His photography centers around the mountains and waterways that surround him, as well as other landscapes in the United States, England and Canada. He is a member of the Adirondack Artists Guild, and his work is held in many private and public collections. His photographs have been honored in both national and regional competitions and have been published in many forms throughout his career.

KEVIN "MUDRAT" MACKENZIE is assistant registrar at St. Lawrence University as well as an Adirondack writer and photographer. An avid outdoorsman whose passion is exploring the backcountry of the Adirondacks in all seasons, he is an official photographer for Adirondack Wildlife and Rehabilitation Center as well as a freelance photographer in the Lake Placid, New York area, where he and his wife, Deb MacKenzie, reside. For further information and photographs, visit www.mackenziefamily. com/46/46r.html or www.mackenziefamily.com/creativenature.

DAVID PYNCHON is an artist from Canton, New York, whose work focuses on capturing people's relationships to place through photography. He is a member of the class of 2014 at St. Lawrence University, where he works as the assistant to the university photographer.

Ohio native LUCRETIA LEONARD ROMEY graduated from Indiana University in 1955 and embarked on a career as a painter, watercolorist, quilter, writer and teacher, winning awards in major national art shows. She lived for several years in Canton, New York, while her husband, Bill, was chair of the Department of Geology and Geography at St. Lawrence University. In 1992 and 2000, she taught art on the University of Pittsburgh's Semester at Sea Program. She illustrated several regional books and published articles in many magazines, including *Adirondack Life*. She passed away in 2012.

KEN WILEY grew up in Brooklyn, New York, and earned his MFA in painting from the University of Iowa. He taught art, photography, pottery and sculpture at North Country Community College for many years. Of *First Snow*, he writes, "As I am a painter of compositions, this scene presented all the elements of one—shapes, textures, lines and shadows, space, and subtle color values. The season's first snow quietly covered the ending fall with a clean blanket."

Visit us at
www.historypress.net
....
This title is also available as an e-book